The NEW Spiritual Chakras

The NEW Spiritual Chakras

and How To Work With Them

Elizabeth Joyce

THE NEW SPIRITUAL CHAKRAS
AND HOW TO WORK WITH THEM
by
Elizabeth Joyce

ISBN: 098980299X
ISBN 13: 9780989802994

Cover Artist:
Evelyn Hart

Books may be ordered through Amazon.com,
booksellers or by contacting:
Visions of Reality
PO Box 128
Chalfont, PA 18914
www.new-visions.com
Printed by Visions of Reality
In the USA

DEDICATION
TO
DANUTA POLICHT

For guiding me through receiving the Divine Seals
and New Spiritual Chakra System

A Universal Gift

The greatest gift
you can give another
Is not fortune or fame,
But knowledge.
To develop himself to
His highest potential.

In all the other Worlds and Universes,
May Love expand throughout!

Also by Elizabeth Joyce

Books

Psychic Attack, Are You A Victim"?
Ascension—Accessing the Fifth Dimension
Ascension—Accessing the Fifth Dimension–Workbook

Opening To Your Intuition and Psychic Sensitivity — Book One
Opening To Your Intuition and Psychic Sensitivity — Book Two
Opening To Your Intuition and Psychic Sensitivity — Book Three

Seeding and Nurturing the Garden of Your Soul

CD Programs

Spiritual Healing and Meditation
Healing Depression the Natural Way
The Chakras and Your Body
Opening the Spiritual Chakras

Contents

List of Graphics

Acknowledgements

I would like to thank Evelyn Hart for her complete dedication to each and every original graphic in this book. She has a sense of knowing exactly what I am picturing, and getting it down on paper.

Thanks go out to Danuta, Theresa Szarawara, Kathy Sasso, and everyone who has supported me in bringing forth this new information. There have been many tests and it has not been an easy path, however the way is cleared to all to open and expand with this new gift from the Universe.

Lastly, gratitude and thanks go to Amritanandamayi, the hugging Saint, for hearing my prayers and allowing this information to enter my thoughts and flow through me, and back out to you, to help raise up, balance, and better the world.

The NEW Spiritual Chakras

and How To Work With Them

Introduction

Is it possible that all the knowledge of the universe is stored within us? Within in the atoms, molecules and cells that becomes our physical living self and each living moment, molded in our genes and DNA? Are we then able to process our cellular memory and DNA automatically and unconsciously with our brain? In this century we have come to believe that it is possible and that there may be a way to "access" this universal knowledge through a lost system which perhaps the ancient *wise men* had developed and applied to answer the fundamental questions: "Who are we? What are we? Where do we come from?"

I believe the answer to further soul development lies between these pages. At least developing our spiritual chakras is a step to knowing and accessing other worlds and universes, finding a way to have compassion, forgiveness, and finally to walk the path of balance, health, fulfillment, helping others, and embracing our differenced without judgment.

Although this information has been with us all along, we are now able to, for the first time in eons, access these energies and apply them to ourselves, which is invaluable to us as well as to others. Perhaps we have found one of the answers to creating harmony within, leading to World Peace!

—Elizabeth Joyce
August 16, 2015

I

Introducing the New Spiritual Chakras

In addition to the normal Chakra Energy System there exists an extended chakra system, the *Spiritual Chakras,* which is just now coming into humanity's awareness. This energy system is latent in most people; however, as more people advance spiritually and begin to ascend and raise their vibrations, this extended energy system begins to unlock the *golden door.* The new system, a natural part of the Fifth Dimension, is the next step in the Spiritual evolution of the planet.

In ancient times, the great Masters, as well as many other teachers along the way, were accessing this powerful energy system. In the past, the Fifth Dimension energies have not been available to all, but only to the chosen few. This energy, originating from the *Double Helix* at the center of our galaxy, arrived on December 21, 2012, and now the time has arrived for others to become aware of these new chakras and reap the rewards of accessing this powerful energy in their daily and spiritual lives.

The present understanding of the *chakra system* gives you seven active and spinning chakras, reaching up the spine from the base of the spine to the crown of the head The two foot chakras, Chakra Zero, is your Earth grounding center and is located at the balls of both feet. Above the Crown Chakra are four more, numbered eight and then ten to twelve. The Ninth Chakra is located at the base of your skull at the back of your head, and the Eight and One—Half Chakra is extended about eight feet out from behind your head, forming a *Triad* between the Eighth and Ninth Chakras.

The main purpose of these extended chakras, which have always been a part of the human energy field, is to enable the individual to tune in to his or her inner God-Self, the Divine Will, the guides and angels, and even the galactic community that surrounds and supports the Earth in its evolution. The first Chakra Group, zero to seven, the *Physical Chakras*, are meant to help you with your development regarding the Earth and the Third Dimension; they help you to become One with the planet. Then, the next five chakras, eight to twelve, help you to become *One with the Universe.*

Your awareness is slowly being moved away from your center, your *physical self*, outward to encompass the larger framework of other people, life forces, other world realities, and divinity itself. In this way, you become more than you were before and more aligned and perfect as well. When you stop focusing on yourself and begin to focus on these larger energies, you move out of your small world and step into a new Universal awareness *where almost anything is possible.* From a reality-creating standpoint this movement to unlimited possibilities is very, very powerful.

This extended Chakra System aids you in the breaking down of the Self within the confines of time and space. To move outward into other dimensions and realities is to come face to face with the idea that the physical Earth is just one place of many that you could have or can inhabit. In the vast regions of the Universe, you have existences that are just as rooted and meaningful as your present earthbound cohabitation is. There are things that you do in these other realities, just like you do here on Earth, and these things are just as significant as your physical lives.

Furthermore, when you begin to glimpse these other realities and see what is happening, a new picture of what is developing begins to take shape. You realize that all your existences are like individual musical instruments in a great orchestra that you are directing and creating. You see yourself as a being that transcends time and the physical body, using your etheric or Universal body instead.

Each Spiritual Chakra, besides aiding in your own energy development and wellbeing, helps you to touch a particular portion of this vast Universe. *Each Spiritual Chakra opens up a corresponding doorway to another portion of the great vastness that is "The Creator".* During the accessing and opening of the Spiritual Chakras process you could become aware of past-lives and places that you may begin to access and identify with. You may also begin to remember and utilize spiritual gifts and talents from the past, and incorporate that learning into your present life.

As in all of nature, there is a natural order to each chakra; the opening of one leads very gently to the opening of the next. Because of this order, these centers will awaken one by one, with each center becoming more alive as another, higher one, begins to spin in harmony and synchronicity with the chakras below.

If you were to observe the openings from a perspective of time, there is a pattern to each opening. Generally, the 8th Chakra Center will open first, located in the Fourth Dimension, with a delay before another expansion occurs. Then, after this delay, in perfect timing, the 8 1/2 Chakra will guide the 9th to open and the 10th will show just a glimmer of activity. At this point, the 8th Chakra Center will expand more. Then, when the 10th Center actually starts to open and spin, the 9th Center will experience another expansion with the 8th Center expanding even further.

The next level or octave will have the 11th Center expanding with the 12th Center showing just a glimmer of activity. Then the process continues, bringing the energy down into the other Chakra Centers forcing them to spin differently and open up more. Luckily, the newest Chakra, the 8 1/2 Chakra, has arrived to filter out this intense energy and protect the body from becoming over- exposed, or from opening up too fast for the lower body system to receive, absorb, and regulate the new vibrations; the 8 1/2 Chakra is filtered by invisible guides and Angels.

Below is a side view of what these NEW chakras look like and where they are placed.

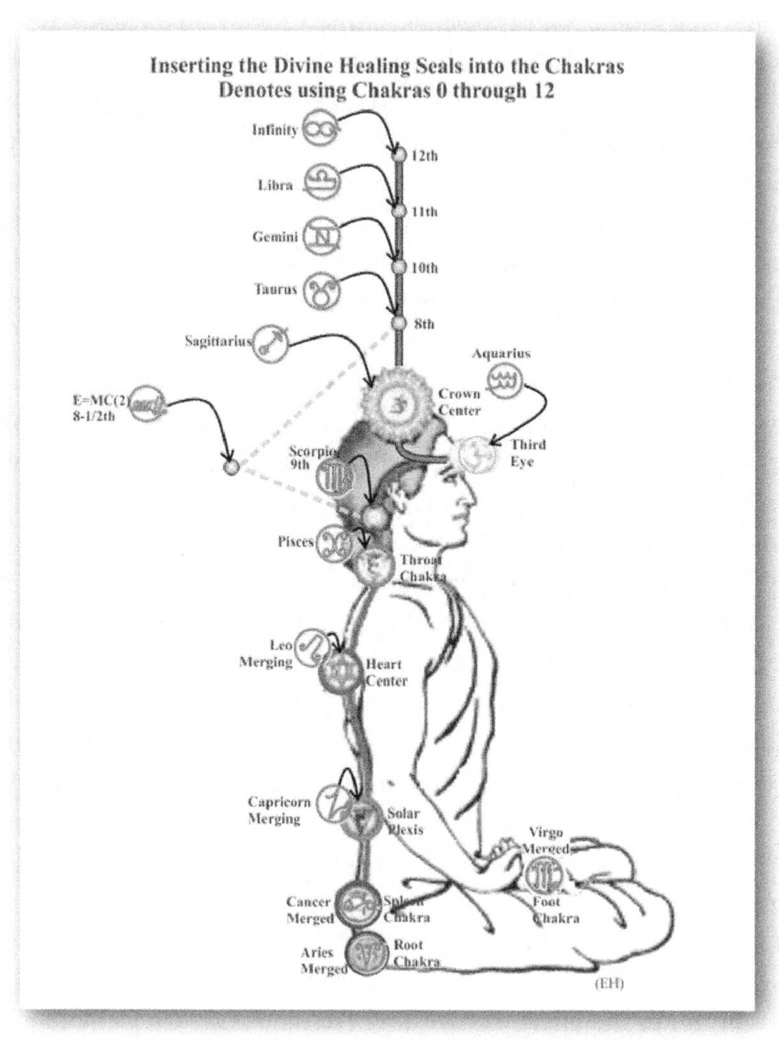

Because of the way these centers awaken, it is a good idea to work with the new spiritual chakra system from the ground up. In this way, the natural awakening of the spiritual senses will take place in correct order, and you will not have to contend with overloading yourself or your clients. From a healing standpoint, this is a good thing to remember. If you are not sure which spiritual centers are active then always clear each center starting from eight and going, in order, up toward twelve.

Working in this manner you will feel increasing body resistance as you approach the Spiritual Chakras that are not yet open. The idea is to avoid opening up a center prematurely, which is difficult to do anyway. Be aware there are several safeguards in place that keep this from happening. Too swift an opening can burn up the brain cells or cause severe mental disorders. But, by gently becoming aware of the vibration of these centers, in time, you will quickly be able to access the individual's spiritual position, know what is going on in that person's life and just how to help them. As you will see, *knowing what Spiritual Chakras are open will give you great insight into what lessons the individual is dealing with.* (See Chart – pg. 101) Unlike the lower centers, there is a plan to their opening and the gifts and lessons that are bestowed on the individual are carefully guided from invisible forces.

Sometimes a particular spiritual chakra will not awaken. Even with the vibrational nature of the spiritual chakra's awakening, it is possible for one to be bypassed. For example, the 9th center could become blocked from opening because of some structural abnormality in the *Soul Blueprint.* When the 10th center begins to awaken, as it will, its energy will flow into the lower centers. If the 9th is blocked, that energy will pass by it and go into the 8th. The 8th will then expand. What you will have is an open 10th center, with a blocked 9th center, and an open 8th center. This causes an imbalance until the 9th Chakra is cleared. This could be one of the reasons we are now experiencing *Divine Headaches.*

Generally, the even numbered centers are fluidic (8th, 10th, 12th) and tend to pass on energy, even if they are closed to some extent. However, they do tend to shut down completely when there is a problem, blockage, or imbalance with them. Once you clear up an even numbered center, it begins to vibrate correctly. You usually do not have to go back into it later on to do more healing.

On the other hand you will find, as the odd numbered centers (9th, 11th) tend to develop, various kinds of blocks will not shut down completely. Unlike an even numbered center, these blocks keep the chakra from operating at full potential or, at the very least, operating strangely. For this reason, you may find that clearing the odd number centers will become more common in your vibrational healing work. By learning what each Spiritual Chakra contains, and its vibration rate, you will know exactly what gifts of the Soul are held back by these blocks.

Remember, the odd Chakra Centers tend to have energetic hardwire problems. In your clearing and restructuring work of a typical odd numbered center, you will literally have to find the improper connection and redirect or rewire it to where it should be flowing. If you are clairvoyant and can see on the finer planes of manifestation, then note that while doing a healing on an odd numbered center, it will look as if you are working on some kind of intricate electronic circuit. You may see what looks like a loose or burned out filament. Then see this filament being removed, and a new one set in to the correct flowing pathway.

These improper connections tend to develop due to the reincarnation process. If a lifetime is not properly cleared, after the Soul has moved on to the next incarnation, certain energy strands do not get wired properly in the rebirth, within these odd numbered Spiritual Chakras. As you evolve through the reincarnation process, you can actually construct and wire up these odd energy centers yourself. This is one of the main purposes of hosting a body here on Earth. With a completely flawless reincarnation cycle, these odd centers assemble in the proper fashion. *Flawless,* in this instance, means a set of incarnations where the lacks of one are properly balanced by the abundances of another.

Typically, when these chakras begin to awaken and spin, they should do what they are supposed to do. However, from improperly cleared lifetimes in the reincarnation cycle, some of these connections can be either left out or wired incorrectly. When these centers begin to open, they misfire and don't start to spin properly. Part of the healing process is to go in and rewire that chakra so that it can operate as it is supposed to. Naturally, the act of rewiring the chakra will release that particular life experience imprint and free the individual from its corresponding chains. *Since the arrival of this new energy in 2012, the past lives of every Soul are coming up for review and thousands of people will be thrown off center. In 2013 thousands of people felt loss and change because of these unbalanced energies.*

This kind of trauma is not your typical life experience material. They are behavior patterns of a multi-lifetime existence. Be aware, this is what will be happening with your clients. For example, reincarnating into a body that has poor circulation time and time again is a sign of an improperly cleared lifetime. In this case example, one of the odd numbered Spiritual centers—most likely the 9th Chakra, the Karmic Blueprint center—has a filament set in the wrong place. This incorrect filament usually shows itself when the individual begins to Ascend and that spiritual chakra begins opening. The removal or the resetting of the improper filament to its correct place will not only restore the chakra, but it will enable the individual to reincarnate in a body more suitable, should that individual reincarnate again. At the very least, it will restore that individual's present body functioning to normal.

If you are not as yet able to etherically *see* the improperly functioning filament, there are mudras that can be used to instruct you exactly on what level and where the malfunction is located, and in exactly what chakra. Permanent and very powerful body healings can be accomplished by working with the odd numbered Spiritual Chakras. These healings are almost always karmic in nature and the individual's life will surely be different after a *Harmonization* and Vibrational healing session.

You can *set a condition* that the 9th Chakra is worked on for clearing during your meditations. This will create a more rapid change in the body, mind, and Soul of an individual that is awakening to his/her spirituality.

This may be uncomfortable for a while, but in truth, is very common because these odd numbered centers are being awakened and many of these improper connections are being reworked and cleared. Prior to this Ascended State, the Universal gift of these new, highly focused energies is the clearing of a particular karmic pattern. Normally, this requires the individual to reincarnate and go through the life process to rewire that filament. However, as the planet evolves and more people come into their higher spiritual awareness, the *Oneness,* these energy centers open up in a natural way. This facilitates a kind of healing and cleansing of the Soul that has not been known or felt throughout this Galaxy for eons.

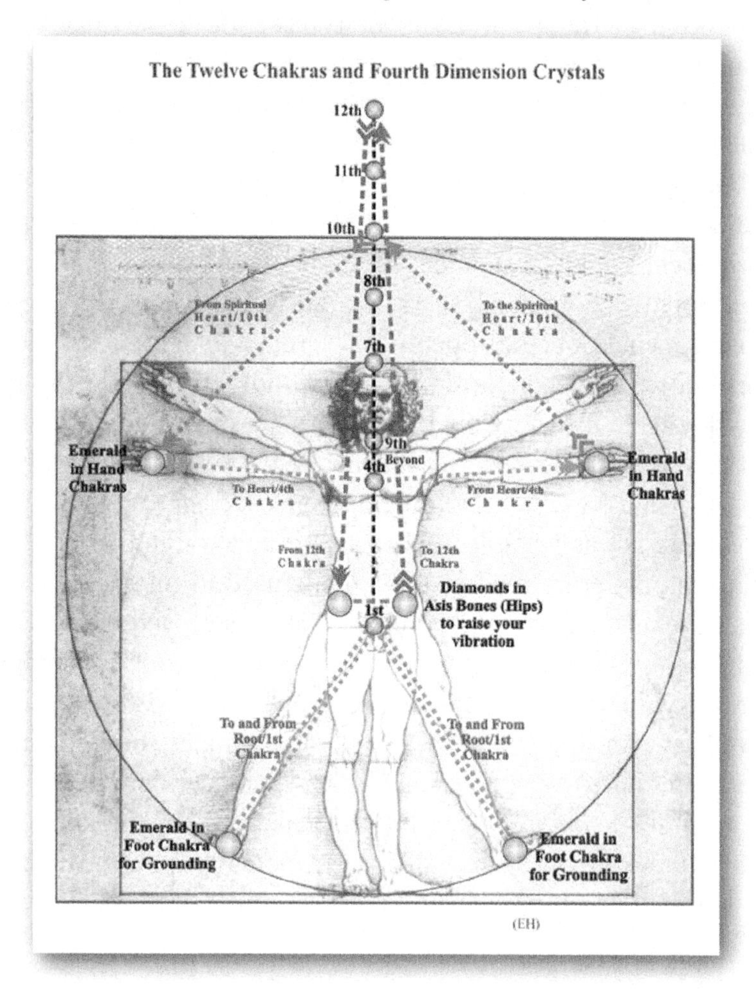

The even numbered Spiritual Chakras (8th, 10th, 12th) are a bit different from the odd numbered ones. These centers deal with fluidic *States of Being.* They also deal with spiritual knowledge and its proper use in the Universe. But more importantly, they are responsible for implementing the programming from the previous chakra. For example, the 8th Chakra is responsible for processing the programs contained in the 7th. The 10th is responsible for processing the programs in the 9th. The 12th is responsible for processing the programs in the 11th. Therefore, when a particular odd numbered center (7th, 9th, 11th) is spinning properly, but there seems to be a problem in getting the individual to implement that proper patterning, then the corresponding higher, even numbered (8th, 10th, 12th) chakras need to be looked at more closely.

If you find that an even numbered chakra has shut down, the cause is most likely from some kind of fear held within the individual. For example, the fear of facing ones karmic residue will cause the 8th center to remain closed. The programs from the 7th Chakra Center will not be able to be implemented, and thus the individual will block the Ascension process. The 7th Chakra Center contains the programs that guide the individual toward Ascension. It is only when an individual is ready to face who and what they are over many lifetimes—that the 8th center will begin to open up. The release of these fears will open the door so that the blocked chakra can open, spin correctly, and allow the programs contained in its odd numbered twin to be implemented and integrated into the entire body system.

The healer needs a good understanding of what each Spiritual Chakra is and its relationship with its twin, to see where the problem/ blockage may lie. For example, if an ascending individual has a fear of leaving the body, this fear will keep the 12th Chakra closed. They will be unable to take advantage of the programs in the 11th Chakra, which deal with the Spiritual path of the Soul, and will not be able to travel with their Universal Body, consciously, outside the body into the galaxy, Universe, and beyond. In this instance, a clearing of this fear will be necessary so the energy center can properly begin its spin. The individual can then project free of the body, and make full use of this ability—walking fully aware in their *Universal Body.*

On the other hand, using the above example again, if that same individual can etherically project out of the body, but is yet unable to travel into the past, then the 12th Chakra is functioning properly. You will know the defect lies in an improperly wired 11th Chakra, which is blocking the individual from being able to travel into the past. A filament in the 11th Chakra is wired improperly, so the individual does not have the proper access to this information. He can travel out of the body, because some of those programs are usable and the 12th center is operating, but he cannot avail himself of that one aspect, *Soul travel into the past.*

As you can see, a clear pattern in diagnosing these spiritual charkas and enabling them to function properly is developing here. As we get into the specifics of each Spiritual Chakra, you will be able to look at a spiritually awakened individual and tell just what chakra has the problem and what the remedy is. In this book we will be getting into the specifics of each Spiritual Chakra, its function, its diagnosis, and the ways to heal and awaken that center.

The Spiritual Chakra System

Chakra 12—Diamond/Crystal Clear

Brings the connection to the Higher Dimensional level of Divinity, advanced spiritual skills, ascension, connection to the Great Masters, our Universe and beyond.

Chakra 11—Aqua Blue/Silver

Opens the pathway to the Soul, the individual's ability to acquire advanced spiritual skills (travel beyond the limits of time and space, teleportation, bi-location, instantaneous precipitation of thoughts, and telekinesis in some cases)

Chakra 10—Bright Yellow/Silver
The Heart Center of the Spiritual Chakras. Brings Divine creativity, synchronicity of life; the merging of the masculine and feminine within, unlocking of skills and higher energies contained in the Ninth Chakra.

Chakra 9—Magenta/Silver
Opens to the Soul Blueprint, the individual Soul's total skills and abilities learned in all the life times.

Contains all karma, knowledge, and actions since the Soul was created.

Interfacing Chakra (8 1/2)—Amber/Mother of Pearl
There is a half-spin chakra between the Eighth and the Ninth Chakra, spinning at a lower rate. This chakra brings a clear triad connection between the Third Eye, Ninth Chakra, and the Crown Center, and it governs emotional and mental clarity. Problems with any of these areas usually show up here, and express themselves as a Fifth Dimensional headache. This Chakra vibrates half in the Fourth Dimension and half in the Fifth Dimension. *It is your bridge to accessing and ascending to the higher levels.*

Chakra 8 – Ultraviolet/Clear
Brings in the new Energy and is the first center of Divine Love rather than physical love, of spiritual compassion, and spiritual selflessness. Your karmic residue activates the Soul's spiritual skills and purification contained in the Seventh Chakra,

Chakra 7—Crown Chakra—Violet/Silver
Traditionally is your connection to the Divine. Contains programs to be used by 8th and 9th Chakras including the release of basic psychic skills, telepathy, seeing auras, lucid dreaming, out-of-body travel, natural energy healing, and feeds this to the 6th Chakra—the Third Eye.

Inter-Dimensional Vibrational Healing™ is the way of the future. This high-level healing is a process whereby vibrations are introduced or transferred into a human being's physical and energetic body. The vibrations that have become unbalanced in the physical or Universal body are adjusted. This is based on the idea that illnesses or diseases in these bodies are characterized by blockage and imbalance. These blockages and imbalances cause a cell, organ, system, or energetic body to slow its vibration. Slow vibrations result in disease (dis-ease) or illness. The process of *Inter-Dimensional Vibrational Healing*™ restores the natural flow to this energy field.

This New Spiritual Chakras book gives you a step-by-step process on how to accomplish this. May you grow, develop, and ascend by using these energies wisely, according to Natural and Divine Law.

Notes on New Spiritual Chakras

Notes on New Spiritual Chakras

II

Fifth Dimension Energy Shifts

Raising your Consciousness

When one lives a life dedicated to raising one's consciousness, that of others, and our planetary culture, it is also a path geared towards the natural healing and harmonization of Self. This is because a higher consciousness is the principle of the *Oneness* connection as it evolves in nature. Since Self-healing is a re-connection, healing and consciousness are inseparable. This is why, when something falls on our head, consciousness immediately rushes there. It is the consciousness of pain.

We can raise our consciousness like we might raise a newborn child. *Love* is the most connective of all emotions and thus love raises consciousness. Integrity of mind, becoming responsible and self-reliant, and not harboring contradictions, enhances the connectivity and unity of our mental terrains. We may raise a child to have integrity of mind and character, and thus, we raise our consciousness. Learning to heal our body, to make it whole, likewise raises consciousness.

Ultimately we uplift our consciousness by being peacemakers and healers as well as by being true to ourselves and each other and planet Earth—with love, compassion, and caring.

We can raise our consciousness to highest levels by developing an overall worldview, by embracing a world that transcends illusions. Doing this will overcome even the final hurdle of inner consciousness—its first shock of separating and the soul split. This is the first duality of the whole of consciousness and manifests in our right/left hemisphere split. How do we transcend that highest of inner rifts? We do so by putting the wisdom of the right hemisphere, its connective consciousness, above the left-brain's lower separation consciousness. The former evolves from realizing, accessing, and opening our new spiritual chakras. The later evolves a purely mathematical, mechanical dominating worldview. We really need to make accessing our higher self our second consciousness, instead of the other way around. Then we can connect what is most separate and harness the mechanical Third Dimension reality for the benefit of our life and those around us. We grow and our consciousness expands as well as our spiritual gifts.

We are now immersed in challenging the root and core paradigm of modern science—that nature functions essentially mathematical. The world is at war on many levels. Chronic disease is on the rise. Violence pervades the Middle East. Animal agriculture is taking a devastating toll on ecosystems everywhere. Economic exploitation has become business as usual. Earthquakes, floods, volcanic eruptions, and other symptoms of climate change are becoming common occurrences. Every twenty minutes another specie of plant or animal becomes extinct. Every year, fifteen million children die of hunger. Proponents of genetically modified foods claim that they can solve this crisis, while hiding data about the destructive effects of these elements on the human body, health, and environments. This has now become serious and dangerous, especially to our children.

In order to know how to "heal consciousness," we first need reliable means to know what it is to "heal" and to have "consciousness" or to become "conscious." A new energy arrived on December 21, 2012, allowing all humans to access the higher dimensions through the NEW spiritual chakras. We need to understand that these new energies are available to everyone on this planet to raise our vibration levels, and hence, raise our consciousness.

How can this be accomplished? All the details are here for you to begin the work. If we do the reverse in a worldview, we yield to mass control, atomic weapons, and chemical pollution. We disconnect from our inner power, from what is whole. We end up with essentially a non-sustainable planetary culture, living in duality and fear.

These are all symptoms of the current *Culture of Death.* What can one do to effectively counterbalance these destructive forces? If consciousness is the permeating essence of life and, our culture upholds a mechanical worldview to yield highest truths, we can logically conclude that guided by the latter we'll create, in time, a *Culture of Death.*

The past four hundred years bear this out. We thus must raise our inner consciousness; you and I, friends and family, to the very highest levels and not just as a mere luxury or recreation, but a real survival necessity. That is why the NEW Spiritual Chakras and understanding their power is so important. It is the key to *Peace on Earth.*

Healing Consciousness

In order to know how to "heal consciousness," we first need a reliable means to know what it is to "heal" and to have "consciousness" or to become "conscious." Then we need to understand that new energies are available on this planet to do exactly that. Raise our vibration levels, and hence, raise our consciousness, or awareness if you prefer. How can this be accomplished?

Energetic Healing

Healing, in one form or another, tends to be a way of connecting something living to the wholeness of the Universe. This is why when a cut mends we say it is healed. Also when a heart is broken and then mends, we say it is healed. The former connects something physically separate. The latter connects something separate in our Spirit. There also can be mental/emotional healing, environmental healing, and so on.

Consciousness

Imagine this—consciousness forms "a potentially universal relationship of connection in all of nature." This is a powerful definition when practically applied. Thus to be "aware" or "conscious" is to know that we simply connect to something we are so aware or conscious of. If this is a reliable and depth insightful definition, then the *very presence of consciousness will tend to mend or heal what is separate.*

Evidence

There is evidence of this. Thus when something falls on our head, for example, and we have a cut or bruise, there also immediately occurs a heightened awareness we call pain. You might cry out, for example, "Oh my God, it hurts." God here is a connective inner cosmic image —trying to pull down the power of healing within—and the experience of pain is also subliminally connected to the connective healing process. This is why many strongly oppose most painkillers or chemical drugs that engender just unconsciousness and therefore interfere with integral emotional and spiritual healing. This phase has two major meanings:

Healing Consciousness can use the word *"healing" as an adjective.* This means consciousness with the characteristic of being healing. But this is actually a redundant phrase, something that is critical to know. Western medicine is grounded in the mechanical, math- based vision of nature. Mathematics shows us how best to separate elements of consciousness; moving our awareness away from the very essence of consciousness itself. This is why machines made of separate, math-delineated or designed parts, tend to be relatively unconsciousness. Also using modern medicines, based as the mechanical model, we can expect trouble with any attempt to heal systemic ailments since there is no science contained for the foundational healing of consciousness.

Healing Consciousness can use the word *"healing" as a verb.* This can mean the mending of our state of consciousness or *State of Being.* Consciousness itself actually can never be healed, as it is the foundation of healing itself. It is rather that our state of incomplete, separate consciousness is what needs to be repaired, mended, reconnected or made whole—brought back into the state of Oneness. This is known as the *State of Being.* Some of us can get to this state once in a while, through meditation techniques, or by being with a Divine Soul. However, our bodies are made to incorporate these higher energies and dwell in the State of Being ongoing, twenty-four/seven.

To do so requires a deeper understanding and creating an advanced inner technology. This technology is now here on the earth. It is being brought in from the Fifth Dimension energies and the Divine Seals presented in *Ascension—Accessing The Fifth Dimension Workbook.*

Healing Our Entire Being

This can be accomplished by intertwining the physical, mental, and emotional parts of ourselves. Actually we have potentially twelve waves of depth and complete healing, beginning with the healing of our state of consciousness—then expanding progressively to transform our mind, emotions, body, immediate family, community, social relationships, and finally our overall connection to our environment and Universe as a whole. It is time for all of us to open up and Ascend by conscious choice.

The following are examples of what many of us are experiencing as the energy shifts to higher vibrationary levels.

Symptoms Of Fifth Dimension Energy Shifts

Headaches:

When the Crown Chakra opens or expands it can be an intense and painful experience. It might feel like a spike or rod is being inserted into the top of your head . Headaches are common and they can range from migraines, to cluster headaches. Women seem to experience them more than men. They can be caused by too much energy flowing through the Crown Chakra, and by hormonal changes, which occur when the chakras are stimulated. Sometimes the pain can be eased by asking Spirit and your Higher Self to make an adjustment in the energy flow.

When you ask for aid to ease the pain and it is part of the process that is opening and expanding your pineal or pituitary gland, the pain will only lessen. As your vibration rate increases, the pineal and the pituitary glands expand to accommodate the higher energy frequencies. Other glands change also, but these two are the major ones that contribute to headaches. This can last a few months, or a few years depending on what level of spiritual development that you are at and your rate of growth.

Flu-Like Symptoms:

This is quite common and part of the process. Just ride it out and don't take antibiotics unless absolutely necessary, which will only prolong the process. These symptoms are caused by the physical reaction to the toxins that are released when the chakras begin to expand. Whatever was constricting or congesting the chakras is flushed through the blood. Also, as new beliefs and paradigms are enacted the imprinted consciousness in the blood becomes toxic to the current physical system because it does not support the new thoughts, and contributes to confusion. It is helpful to supplement the body with blood fortifying enzymes, herbs, and essential oils to ease the symptoms. Hot lemon drinks will also help cleanse the body. Don't work too much during this time, because you are going through a major shift in vibration. Try and take it easy and it will pass.

Nausea, Loose Bowel Movements, Diarrhea:
This is a common reaction when the Solar Plexus Chakra opens and releases the stored fear, anger and resentment held in the area. Karmic and family issues will produce gas and farting. The Bach Flower Rescue Remedy can ease these symptoms. Don't be afraid to take it every thirty minutes if necessary.

Muscle Aches and Joint Pain:
Increasing your vibration forces the energy through the body. When there are blockages impeding the energy flow this raised and forced energy slams into them causing the blockages to break apart as well as these symptoms and ails. Often this is alleviated by asking for assistance from the Higher Self to adjust the flow to ease the pain. The body can quickly adjust to the higher vibration in a few moments, hours, or days.

Depression:
A very common symptom caused by an increased rate of vibration. This higher frequency forces any illness, virus, or infection hiding in the body to surface. To discover the root- cause contributing to this state, examine your beliefs and decisions that are creating your reality. It is also important to monitor your internal dialogue to learn what you are creating for yourself. Observing and realizing that the state you are experiencing is not caused by the present allows it to quickly pass. The herb "St. Johns Wart" eases depression and is anti-viral too.

Crying for no Reason, Feeling Emotionally Vulnerable:
When blockages from this lifetime and other lifetimes begin to release, the emotional body will react in this manner. This new energy stimulates and contributes to the spontaneous release of these burdens. Trying to control or resists these urges further represses and blocks the energy, making things more difficult. Crying, moaning, sobbing, or toning becomes a cleansing release. Use a Bach flower remedy, or an essential oil to help with the emotional body.

Fluttering, Pain in the Heart Area, or Breathing Problems:
This is a symptom experienced when the Heart Chakra begins to open or enlarge to receive more energy. Pain sensations in the heart and not being able to breathe can be very frightening because you may think you are having a heart attack. The above symptoms are caused by the expansion of energy running through your solar plexus and Heart Chakra, the heart and stomach area of the body. The best solution is to relax, which will adjust the energy flow. Anxiety and fear only constrict the energy, thus causing a more severe reaction. This is a normal experience when undergoing a frequency increase.

Hot Flashes and Night and Day Sweats:
These are commonly experienced by both men and women. This is due to energy flowing too quickly through the body, hormonal changes, which men have too, and the body learning to adjust to the higher vibratory rate. Some men might experience fat being stored in this area which may feel like they are growing breasts. If you are a man don't be concerned because this puffiness in the chest area will only last for a short while.

Extreme Tiredness:
Waking in the morning and struggling to get out of bed after a full night of sleep, or falling asleep in the middle of the afternoon is common. This is caused when the energy is shifting throughout the entire physical and spiritual body. This will pass in time and each individual has a different time frame; for some it can be weeks, for others months, for others, years. If you can create a pyramid structure to sit under this will give you wonderful boosts of energy when you are lacking it. Drink lots of pure water to hydrate the cells, add crystals to energize the water. Eat light meals with organic veggies. Doing light physical exercise will stimulate the energy flow through the body as well as *the I AM Meditation* as taught by Amritanandamayi. Bach remedies, flower essences and essential oils will also help the transition.

Excessive Energy:
You go to bed early, exhausted, but in a couple of hours you are wide awake. This is caused by the new energy accumulating around you. This is because of the body's inability to store the energy while it is blocked and congested. It is important not to get up and be active because the energy is for healing all the subtle bodies spiritual, mental, emotional and physical, the best way to assimilate the energy is to quietly sit and read, watch TV, or listen to meditation tapes to help you go back to sleep. This might seem to occur nightly for some time.

Weight Gain:
This is a very common complaint. The body feels like it is being invaded so it adds a layer of protection. If you are a Lightworker, then additional water is needed to create energy. If you don't have enough water, the body will store water, which ultimately leads to stagnation. Another major factor is that with the activation of new DNA, fat is needed to hold the vibration. Body fat holds a higher vibration which is necessary to generate healing and channeling energy. Many of you also have agreed to anchor grids of Light in the areas surrounding where you live.

Anchoring these grids require body fat to help hold the energy. Body fat serves a very loving purpose as it allows embodiments to assist mother earth in holding her vibration. In becoming crystalline, the body fat is evenly distributed around every cell within the embodiment. This allows the entire body to act as a tuning fork to hold a new vibration.

Losing your Memory or Feeling Spacey:
This can be a frightening experience because you cannot remember what you had for dinner, and dinner was only an hour ago. *You are not losing your memory.* You are changing over from left-brain function to more of a right-brain function. Areas of the brain are activated to cope with the higher energy coming in. Sometimes it is hard to speak, words come out jumbled or garbled. This situation will pass, although there is no time limit.

Extreme Sensitivity:
As you open up to the higher vibration, you will find yourself becoming extremely sensitive to people, noises, light, smells, tastes, all sorts of things. This can affect the central nervous system and be quite a difficult thing to cope with. You need to take B vitamins and a multi-vitamin if this is happening to you. If you are allergic to these vitamins then look for a homeopathic remedy or a Bach flower remedy for extreme sensitivity.

Blowing Light Bulbs and Electronics:
If this is happening to you, then you are really reaching a very high vibratory rate and will probably be a profound healer or channel for Spirit. It is due to extremely high energy coming into the physical form. It could be described as 50,000 volts of electricity coming in at once, not only can the body not cope, but it goes through the body and out again and as it does so it affects all electronic equipment within your immediate area.

Animal Reactions:
You will find that dogs, cats and other animals will become aware of your energy and either be frightened of it or want to be around it all the time. Many animals can't get enough of the energy. Others are somewhat frightened because they do not understand it.

Good Changes:
As you vibrate higher, you will find that you no longer want the things that you used to. Coffee, tea and meat are just three of the dietary changes that people make as they begin to vibrate faster. Meat is especially dense and can really affect the body's energy, especially if it has hormones in it. You may develop cravings for certain foods, or go off your favorite foods. This is normal and a part of the change to the higher vibration. If you find this happening, then let it happen and explore the new possibilities.

Our ancestors used miracles to change what they believed. The energy to do this came from the Fifth Dimension. Today we use science, and the combination of both, which, when used in harmony, opens the door to a powerful new way of seeing the world. Now science can explain much of why this is possible, because we have learned that we are *not limited* by the laws of physics and biology. This Ascension work teaches us how to speak the quantum language of healing, peace, abundance, and create change. We can now learn and experience how to make the simple shift in belief that catapults us beyond the limitations of our past.

Once we become aware of these life-altering discoveries, we must think of ourselves differently. The key to Vibrational Healing is to understand what belief is and how it works. This work shows us all of the levels we need to process through in order to ascend. The Hierarchy invites you to embrace this Divine Shift and live beyond the paradigm of false limits.

With the winds that shall come to change that which needs changing, understand and know and trust that every one of those light particles that you part with, that are drawn off of your body system by others who are racing to come up levels in their healing and ascension process, will go forth transforming other's lives, and with that knowledge we realize that not now or ever, can we be alone.

The Earth is now knee-deep in an economic meltdown. Every day you hear reminders of the ailing financial systems of key countries such as Greece, Egypt, China, and the United States. On a personal level, you likely have your own reminders of the fragile nature of the economic infrastructure of your now global society. You have learned to depend upon these financial systems, and to expect that they would always be there in the familiar forms. All that structures is now changing.

To be sure, it's a big wakeup call to discover that what you once thought reliable and strong is indeed crumbling beneath your feet. There is a natural feeling of loss associated with this, regardless of how you are personally impacted right now. This feeling of loss can be overwhelming, and it can trigger a sudden episode of depression. Even if you don't typically become depressed you can feel like a black cloud is obscuring your happiness, hopes, and dreams.

While comparisons are being made between this current crisis and America's great depression of the 1930's, today's economic predicament is quite different. The world has reached a tipping point, and the out-of-balance structures will need to be addressed in order for humanity to move forward. Band-Aid's will no longer suffice. The global distress cannot be resolved through local measures that are isolationist, protectionist, or elitist.

What you are witnessing and experiencing is part of the great reconfiguration underway as humanity births a new world. Finances are coming under the spotlight first, as this area is closely interconnected with society's other outmoded structures. This crisis is really not personal, yet it certainly can feel very personal when your income, bank account, and even your sense of long term financial security appear to be uncertain. Separate from this, of course, you may well have suffered economic losses on a number of fronts since 2008.

In addition, you may be dealing with a variety of other types of loss, some already manifest and some possible in the conscious fears of the unknown. You may feel anxiety when contemplating the prospect of how much really needs to change on the planet. However, a wise part of you knows that change and loss are normal elements of the creation process on Earth. You likely have witnessed or directly experienced countless losses—big and small—throughout your life. Most likely, you have developed coping mechanisms for handling loss. Some of these you may be aware of, and others may be unconscious.

Your Blessed Higher Self also knows that the changes happening on the planet are a part of the great shift in consciousness predicted to occur at this exact time. The changes came after the galactic energetic shift in 2012. You have come to witness and be a part of this birth. The road now is indeed rocky, yet where it leads is a place in which you as a being can soar!

Below are ten steps you can take to begin to raise your vibration levels and frequencies. We will now work on understanding the Spiritual Chakras, one by one, as well as explaining the application of these powerful centers

Ten Steps to Raising Your Vibration

Raising your vibration is the only effective way to get to the life you truly want to live. While you are emitting a low vibration or frequency your life will never really be in harmony and you will constantly live with an inner feeling of discontent. It is this life of discontent that you have put up with and accepted that keeps you in a state of low vibration. When you find the courage to do something about your low quality of life and choose to make things better, you are on the right track to raising your vibration. Raising your vibration comes down to many factors. Listed below are ten key steps that will definitely help towards raising your vibration immediately.

1. Be mindful of your thoughts, when raising your vibration.

It is imperative to keep a close eye on the habitual thoughts that enter your head. It can be difficult at first to be aware of the many thoughts that constantly bombard your mind all day long, but by beginning to notice unwelcome or negative thoughts, you can start to replace them with a positive thought you already have pre-programmed in your mind. This works wonders towards raising your vibration. When I say pre-programmed, I mean you have a positive thought in your mind, a thought that you know makes you happy, that you substitute in place of any negative thought that comes into your mind. Sometime these are called affirmations.

The key to this thought substitution is to spend more time thinking positive thoughts and less time thinking negative thoughts. Spending more mental time in the positive will help raise your vibration. Suggestion, go to Louise Hay's website (http://www.louisehay.com/) and learn how to do this. Work with her affirmations on a daily basis and write some of your own.

ENERGY DESCENDING FROM THE HIGHER SPIRITUAL CHAKRAS

2. Only talk about what you want, not what you do not want, when looking to raise your vibration.

If you are looking for a new relationship, don't say things like, *I can never find the right person for me.* If you talk this way, it's exactly what you will get and you will make your quest towards raising your vibration that much harder. You always receive back whatever you say and think. Even if you haven't been too successful in finding the right person previously, it does not matter. Change your words and you will change your experiences by what you manifest in your life. Instead say something like, *"It is wonderful that I have found the perfect person for me."* Have a confident expectation that at any time you could meet this person and you will exponentially increase your chances of finding him or her. The same thing goes for money. Do not talk about not having enough money. Either do not talk about it at all or only talk positively about having money, because what you declare comes to you, and money will begin to flow in as you change your thoughts. Try this phrase, *"Money comes to me, flows through me, and back out to do the good."* This will help with raising your vibration as you become stronger. You'll soon begin to feel better about yourself.

3. Stay away from negative or pessimistic people.

These types of people are running at a very low vibration and their low vibration can have a negative impact on your vibration, bringing you down to their level. Instead of raising your vibration, you will lower it and this will bring about more experiences residing in a low vibration level, such as problems, stress, and worry.

4. Spend some time not thinking.

Yes that is right, stop thinking so much. To do this, take a walk through the park or away from the city and noise. Go to a place in the country if you can and take a long walk, concentrating on your surroundings, keeping your mind off your usual thoughts. This is a great way to clear your head and also helps in raising your vibration. If you cannot get away, try listening to some soothing music, such as *Ardas* by the

Crimson Collection, and avoid thinking by concentrating on the vibration, tones, and sounds.

5. Join groups of like-minded people.

Spend time with people interested in the same things you are and learn at the same time. Before I started writing, I took a community college course in writing. Not only did I improve my writing, I also spent time with other people who shared a similar interest. I always walked away from each class feeling positive about being a writer and this had a positive effect on my vibration as it made me feel good about myself. Being around like-minded and positive people seriously helps towards raising your vibration and the vibration levels of those around you.

6. Give away something you can afford each week.

Give away your time and money to a charity you believe in or give away something you don't use anymore but may be useful to someone else. What you give is what you get in life, so by giving you will receive in one way or another. Help others and you will be helped. This is Natural Law. You have a profound effect on raising your vibration when you help others and it makes you feel good from the inside.

7. Be aware of your actions.

Everything you do comes back to you in some way, so always be wary of how you treat others and how you act in all situations. How you treat others is how you will be treated. Doing the right thing by everyone you come in contact with helps towards raising your vibration as others continue to do the right thing by you. Treating everyone well and with respect will have a positive effect on attracting new people and opportunities into your life.

8. Avoid the television, radio and media in general.

It is especially important to avoid all news programs as they do much more harm to your vibration level than they do good. By watching TV, you end up taking in so much negative energy it becomes confusing to your subconscious mind and some of that negative imagery and energy gets absorbed by your subconscious. This elevates a feeling of fear from within. Most of the media works by fear mongering, they want to shock you into a state of fear so you keep on watching and the more you watch the more addicted you become to the fear. This has a disastrous impact on your vibration level and will never have positive effect on raising your vibration. In fact, it could prevent it.

9. Stay optimistic at all times if your goal is to raise your vibration. This can be difficult to do, especially when you are in a crisis, but when you are in a crisis situation, it is most important to stay positive. By remaining positive you keep your vibration high, and when you are vibrating at a higher rate your problems will dissipate so much quicker, you may find it was not really a problem at all. Positive vibrations and events are attracted to positive people. Surrounding yourself with positive, supportive people is a great way to remain in a positive state of mind.

10. Stay in touch with your feelings and emotions.
This is the most important factor in keeping your vibration level high. Your feelings are the cosmic glue with regard to your entire life. When you feel good about yourself only other things residing on the same good frequency will be attracted into your life. Your level of vibration runs parallel with your emotions and feelings, meaning you are in control of your life and the events that come into your life at any given moment. If there is one key factor in relation to raising your vibration it would be to stay on top of your feelings and never allow yourself to feel negative or pessimistic. The better you feel about yourself and your life the higher you will raise your vibration. Remember, emotions are important. Logic is important, but emotions are more important.

Notes on Fifth Dimension Energy Shifts

III

Integrating the Spiritual Chakras

An Overview

Besides the normal Chakra Energy System there exists an extended chakra system, which is just now coming into humanity's awareness. This energy system is latent in most people; however, as more people advance spiritually, this extended energy system begins to unlock the *Golden Door* into the higher realms. This extended Chakra system, a natural part of the Fifth Dimension, is the next step in the spiritual evolution of the planet. Once, a long time ago, the Great Masters of Atlantis and our spiritual Masters along the way, were of the few to access and use this powerful energy system. Now, the time has come for others to become aware of this system and reap the rewards of using it in our daily and spiritual lives.

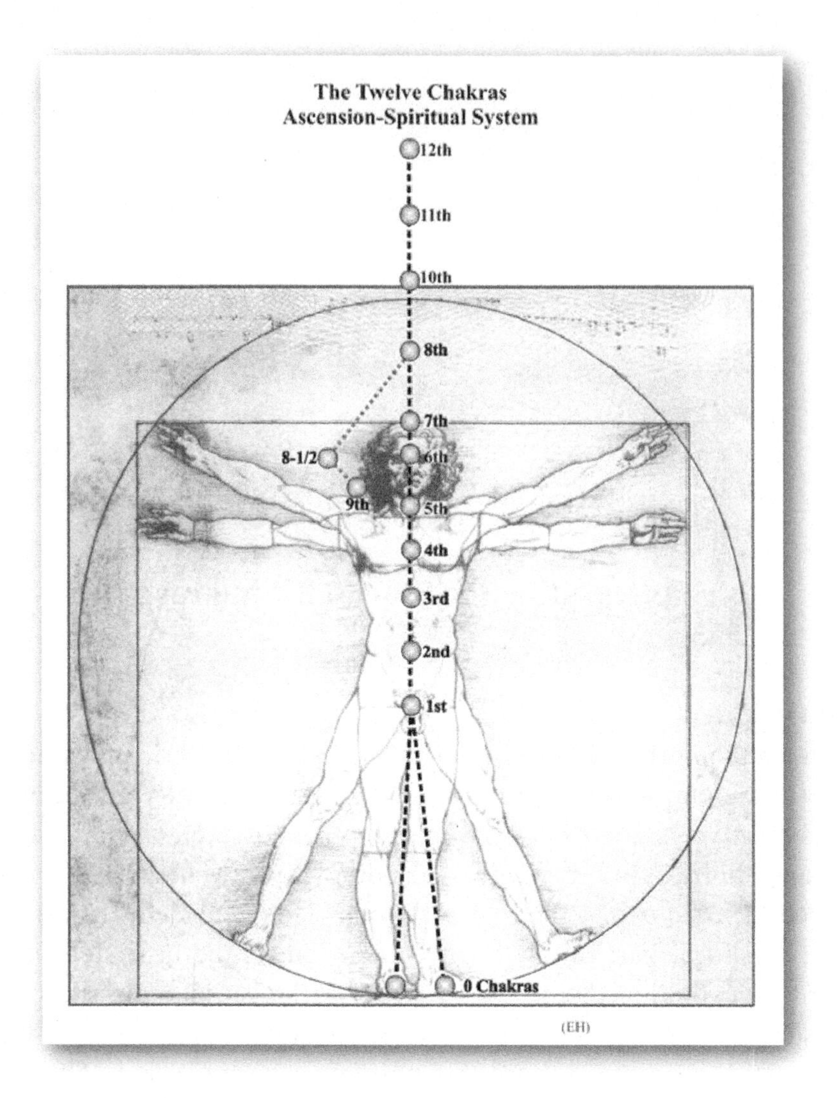

The Twelve Chakras

Chakra 12 - Connection to the Higher Dimensional level of Divinity; brings advanced spiritual skills, Ascension, connection to the High Masters, the Universe and beyond.
Color – Diamond Clear

Chakra 11 - Pathway to the Soul, the individual's ability to acquire advanced spiritual skills; brings the ability to travel beyond the limits of time and space, teleportation, bi-location, instantaneous precipitation of thoughts, telekinesis in some cases. Color – Deep Indigo to Aqua Blue

Chakra 10 - Divine creativity, synchronicity of life; brings the merging of the masculine and feminine within, unlocking of skills and higher energies contained in the Ninth Chakra
Color - Brilliant Yellow/Amber

Chakra 9 - Soul Blueprint, the individual's total skills and abilities learned in all the life times, contains all karma, knowledge, and actions since the Soul was created.
Color – Magenta/Silver

Chakra 8 - Energy center of Divine Love, of spiritual compassion, and spiritual selflessness; holds your karmic residue and activates any spiritual skills and purification contained in the Seventh Chakra.
Color – Clear – Ultra Violet

Chakra 7 – Crown Chakra, traditionally your connection to the Divine contains programs to be used by 8th and 9th Chakra including the release of basic psychic skills; telepathy, seeing aura, lucid dreaming, out of body travel, healing—and feeds this to the 6th Chakra – the Third Eye.

Color – Violet/Silver
The present understanding of the chakra system gives you seven plus one (foot to crown). The extra chakra (Chakra Zero) is your Earth-grounding center, and it is located in the balls of your feet. Now, above the Crown Chakra are four more, numbered eight to twelve. The main purpose of these extended charkas, which have always been a part of the human energy field, is to enable the individual to tune in to his or her inner God-Self, the Divine Will, and even the galactic community that surrounds and supports the Earth in its evolution

The first Chakra Group (zero to seven) helps you with your development regarding the Earth, the Third Dimension; they help you to become One with the planet and keep you grounded. Then, the next five (eight to twelve) help you to *become One with the Universe.* Your awareness is slowly being moved away from your center, your own physical self, and working outward to encompass the larger framework of other people, life forces, realities, and divinity itself. In this way, you become more than you were before and more perfect, too. As you stop focusing on yourself and begin to focus on these larger, expanded energies, you move out of your small world and step into a new area, the entire Universe where anything is possible. From a reality-creating standpoint, this movement in possibilities is very, very powerful.

One of the things that the extended chakra system aids in is the breakdown of the Self within the confines of time and space. To move outward into other dimensions and realities is to come face to face with the idea that the physical Earth is just one place of many that you could have or can inhabit; other places in the more vast regions of the Universe. You may have existences in other parts of the Universe that are just as rooted as your present earthbound cohabitation.

There are things that you do in these other realities, just like you do here on Earth, and these things are just as significant as your physical lives. Furthermore, when you begin to glimpse these other realities and see what is happening, a new picture of what is developing begins to take shape. You realize that all your existences are like individual musical instruments in a great orchestra that you are directing and creating. You see yourself as a being able to transcend time and the physical body.

Each Spiritual Chakra, besides aiding in your own energy development and wellbeing, helps you to touch a particular portion of this vast Universe. *Each Spiritual Chakra opens up a corresponding doorway to another portion of the great vastness that is "The Creator".*

There is a natural order to each chakra in that the opening of one leads very gently to the opening of the next. Because of this ordering, these centers will awaken one by one, as your body allows, with each center becoming more alive as another, higher chakra, begins to spin in synchronicity with the charkas below it.

There is a pattern to this opening, if you were to observe it from a perspective of time. Generally, the 8th Chakra Center will open first, which remains in your aura field in the Fourth Dimension, with a delay before another expansion occurs. Then, after this delay, the 9th will open, hooking you into the new Fifth Dimension energies with the 8 1/2 Chakra acting as a protective filter, and, once opened, the 10th will show just a glimmer of activity. At this point, the 8th Chakra Center will expand more. Then, when the 10th Center actually starts to open, the 9th Center will experience another expansion with the 8th Center expanding even further. The next level or octave will have the 11th Chakra Center expanding with the 12th Center showing just a glimmer of activity. Then the process repeats, spinning in harmony with the lower Spiritual Chakras. It's a kind of wave effect, with each center opening up and waving its vibration and energy down into the other centers, enabling them to open up and expand.

Now let's take a look at each one of the new Spiritual Chakras and how they work, one by one.

Notes on The Spiritual Chakras

IV

The Eighth Chakra

The first of the Spiritual Chakras, numbered Eight, sits above the 7th Chakra about eight feet. It is the energy center of Divine love, spiritual compassion, and spiritual selflessness. It also is the chakra that holds your *karmic residue*—those energy patterns that you have held on to for more than one lifetime. When the Eighth Chakra begins to open up and expand, a new, deeper spiritual awareness begins to take shape within you. You begin to sense yourself as part of a larger community of people. *This chakra is the gateway to other ideas, concepts, and abilities that are new for you.*

This center enables the individual to achieve out-of-body projection, spiritual perception, and spiritual wisdom. *Spiritual Chakras* show you that these abilities and ideas are larger than the Self and the Earth. Their energies go beyond the planet, solar system, galaxy, and perhaps even the Universe. This energy is concerned with healing of the planet and the Self with regard to the Universe and becoming ONE with the ALL-THAT-IS vibration.

You may not understand why the Eighth Chakra center holds your karmic residue, so let's explore this a bit, because when you get into the healing aspect of this chakra you will need to understand its significance. This center is the gateway to your Blessed Higher Self as it expands past the planet. *The Eighth Chakra is the last energy center that holds anything human within it. It, therefore, becomes the temple of human cleansing and the releasing of patterns that are lifetimes old and worn out.* The Bible quote, *"Do you not know that your body is the Temple of the Holy Spirit who is in you, whom you have received from God? You are not your own."* (1 Cor. 6:19) expands into the Universe and enforces the thought that we are a part of the *I Am Oneness.* These karmic patterns are the last strings of what holds you to the reincarnation system and your humanness, which prevents you from uniting with higher powers, beings, and ideas.

When this center opens up, you not only begin to take on an awareness of this larger community of energies, but you begin to shed those patterns that have kept you rooted to the planet Earth, and this Solar System. This shedding is a natural process, as once this center is awakened, the individual is ready to let go of his/her humanity and grasp onto something larger, much more wonderful, and infinitely Divine. Usually this cycle begins when you are in the last level of the Fourth Dimension, or as you enter the first level of the Fifth Dimension.

Because of this strong karmic connection with the body, when the Eighth Chakra Center opens, it is not without duress. *How much friction is encountered will depend on what the individual has to let go of.* It is said that once you open the door to Spirit you are forever changed and can't go back. Well, the opening of this chakra and all its goodies is where the saying comes from. Once the 8th Chakra opens, you become aware of yourself as part of the Universe and not just a part of your small corner of the world. You start to become aware of information on new levels of awareness and intuition. You have to let go of those old outworn human ideas about yourself and the planet, this is the first *shock*, and how you handle this depends on your Soul character, who you are, and how well you take to change. Many people coming for the Spiritual Intensives are working at the 8th Chakra level.

Also, at the same time that you have to deal with all this new information about yourself and the Universe, you have to deal with new body sensitivities and new psychic abilities. These new abilities and awareness can make you feel alienated and ungrounded from the planet, for a time, until the natural grounding in the Foot Chakra opens up and reseats the individual. For this reason, a good Foot Chakra cleansing would be a great way to help an individual that is exhibiting the eighth center coming alive. The Reconnection (Dr. Eric Pearl) leads to the opening of the Eighth Chakra and Foot Chakra, which does not open until the Eighth Chakra begins its spin. That's it for the Reconnection—which is why the I AM Meditation has been put into place by Amritanandam ayi (Amma). The I AM Meditation works on opening up the Tenth Chakra and above—the Spiritual Intensives take you up to the Tenth Chakra Spin-Opening and a bit beyond: creating an overlap.

It is important for healers to be aware that *because karma is involved here*, any kind of vibrational healing that can bring out and clear past life trauma or patterns will help the individual. However, keep in mind that as soon as you clear away any of these old patterns, the individual will experience an acceleration in spiritual abilities. It would be a good idea, in a week or so after such a healing, to follow up with a Foot Chakra clearing to facilitate the passing of these more intense residue energies.

Try to schedule a healing right after taking an Intensive, within three days if the client tells you they were uncomfortable in the body or had a difficult time sleeping or an uncomfortable time after their sitting. As this Eighth Chakra clears, the individual will pass through more spiritual energy

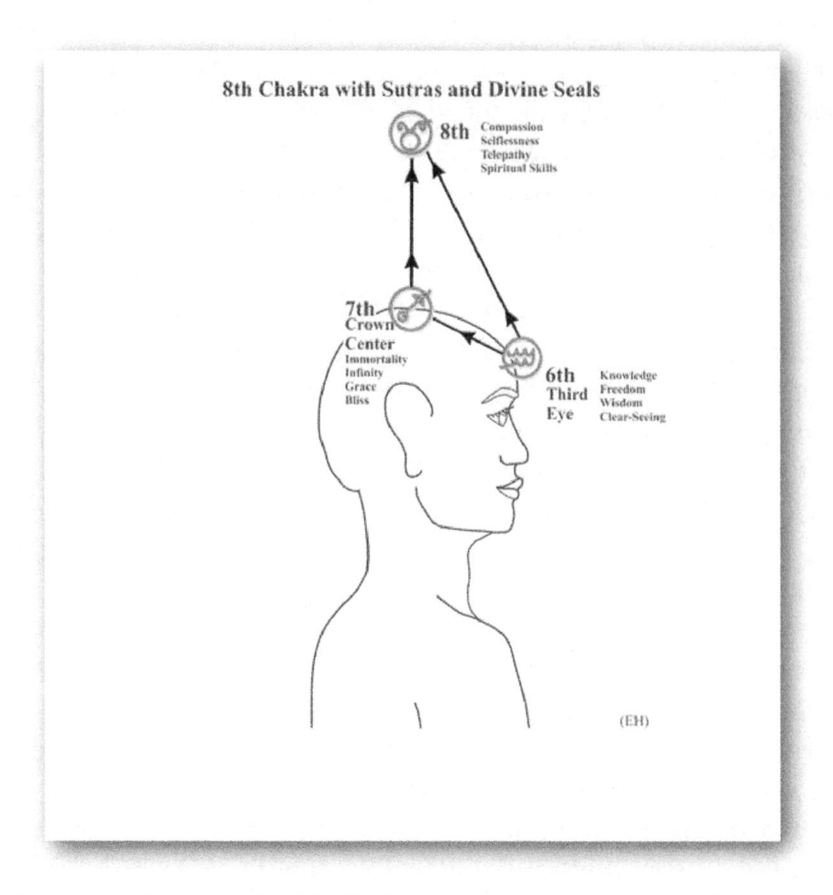

For example, when the 8th Chakra opens, one may start to have out-of-body travels and even be able to command them. Advanced, out of body travel skills, like traveling out of the solar system, traveling backward or forward in time, remembering life on other planets or within another galaxy, will not show themselves until the 11th or 12th Chakra begins to open.

The healing treatment necessary here is to advise the individual that they are not going crazy, but that their latent psychic and spiritual abilities are just starting to open. Advise them to look at these new gifts as a kind of Spiritual awakening and teach them how to accept this in a very simple manner. Meditation of the Spiritual Chakras will help here, as well as the Spiritual Chakra Invocation. (pg. 103) Clearing fear out of the 8th Chakra can greatly help the individual's acceptance, understanding and Ascension, if these abilities seem to be causing any great duress.

Also, the 8th Chakra holds much of one's karmic residue. The newly ascending individual will have to work through and shed some of this karma so that the other higher-level Chakra centers can awaken. Helping the individual understand that they may be dealing with karmic issues and that these concerns need to be addressed, can release much tension, fear, or even erase the karma itself. Again, a good clearing of the 8th Chakra will help here, especially if the karma to be cleared is very old residue that has already been repaid and is just lying around, as is often the case. This karma would naturally clear over time, but the clearing process can be quickened by a professional healer or by doing personal healing work on the 8th Chakra.

δ

Spiritual Chakras Meditation

Close your eyes and visualize yourself standing amidst the most rainbow-like beautiful energy.

Take a deep breath.

Visualize yourself standing in the most beautiful amber-golden mist. It is important to feel very comfortable within this golden energy that takes on the shape of your energy field, beginning to rise up and connect you to your Spiritual Chakras.

Take a deep breath.

See within your mind your Blessed Higher Self – your *Universal Body Self,* contained within the four levels of your Aura, and with that vision—claim yourself to be a powerful being by repeating the *Ascension Invocation for the 8th and 9th Chakra within your mind.* Claim yourself as a powerful healer, creator, and co-creator of this world, working alongside the ***One that Creates All***; co-create your life, your miracles and your preferred existence upon this plane.

Take a deep breath.

Activate this beautiful amber/golden energy that you are enveloped in as you draw within the power and the strength to practice your intention by accepting the higher energetic vibrations and moving into a whole new power of thought by allowing the Divine will of the Supreme God Light to be integrated into your entire Universal Being.

Take a deep breath.

Now imagine a most beautiful silver energy manifest on the inside of the amber/golden energy, insulating the three original levels of your Aura, providing your amber/golden shield with a liquid silver energy.

Take a deep breath.

Remind yourself that you are an expression of fluid love as you become the flow of unconditional love towards the Self and all others. Remind yourself of the feminine aspect of the Universal Body that always supports you in the highest and best way for you to remain flexible, and in so doing, embrace *the Fifth Dimension harmonies*, the flexible side of your personality, by allowing the Creative God Light to create within you the energetic vibration that is needed for you to transform your life.

Take a deep breath.

Now connect your heart center energy to the silver and amber/golden energies. If you need to place your hand on your heart to connect to the reality of your pulsating heart do so.

Take a deep breath.

Now imagine a most beautiful silver energy manifest on the inside of the amber/golden energy, insulating the three original levels of your Aura, providing your amber/golden shield with a liquid silver energy.

Take a deep breath.

Remind yourself that you are an expression of fluid love as you become the flow of unconditional love towards the Self and all others. Remind yourself of the feminine aspect of the Universal Body that always supports you in the highest and best way for you to remain flexible, and in so doing, embrace *the Fifth Dimension harmonies*, the flexible side of your personality, by allowing the Creative God Light to create within you the energetic vibration that is needed for you to transform your life.

Take a deep breath.

Now connect your heart center energy to the silver and amber/golden energies. If you need to place your hand on your heart to connect to the reality of your pulsating heart do so.

Now connect your heart energy to the heart of your etheric plasma, the Universal Body, thus connecting your beating heart to the amber/ gold and silver lining around your aura, attached to the 9th Chakra at the back of your head. You do this by sending unconditional love into this area— the part of your physical reality forming your etheric outline— therefore with every beat of your heart send unconditional love into the spaces that exist between the spaces that surround you. Fill your aura with this amber/ gold and silver light. Send this light-love vibration to fill up all of the particles of light that exists between your non-and-physical localities.

Take a deep breath

Visualize your energy field filling up with light and love as you to visualize your entire aura also filling with a soft pink light. The amber/gold layer is on the outside of your auric energy field, and the silver layer on the inside edge of the fourth level of your aura. Allow the pink Amma energy to fill up your energy field as it carries this light frequency and sound of unconditional love. Allow it to infiltrate your etheric – Universal anatomy, as you to float within the most exquisite and most beautiful plasma of unconditional love.

Begin to visualize that the amber/golden energy that encapsulates the outside of your energy field is sending triggers of energy toward your inner heart pulse. (4th Chakra) It's an energy that creates a sonic vibration of sacred sound and light as it births two golden spheres of energy that float from the 9th Chakra and come to lodge within your Heart and Root Chakra. The amber/golden vibration of your Universal Light Body gives of itself—creating a new golden energy star template lodged within your Heart and Root Chakras.

Take a deep breath.

You are now connecting with every Angelic and Archangelic energy known and unknown to you at the level of your Heart and Root Chakras. Please understand that the time has come for you to *let go of the control you have over others by allowing them to let go of the control they have over you.* Begin to live through your heart, and make a point of shining your light towards others no matter their response. Connect to the *love crystals at the Heart Center,* allowing these energies to transform all of the energy that prevents you from claiming your magnificence as an Angelic Fifth Dimensional Human.

Allow the blame and judgment that passes to you, even by those you hold close, to wash over you and slide away and set the intent at this level of your awareness to have absolutely all negativity transmuted by the Angels of Light.

Release this amber/golden orb of energy from the Root allowing it to travel upwards through your Crown Chakra lodging itself into your 8th Chakra.

Take a deep breath.

At this level, is there anything that you can think of while dwelling within this energy that makes you feel uncomfortable? Now is the time to take note of and work with it. It is a misplaced filament.

Take a deep breath.

Allow this angelic amber/golden orb to ascend—lodging itself within your solar plexus. Using this energy at this level to help you make friends with all of the aspects of the Universal self you still feel incongruent with. Allow this energy to bring into balance all that is needed for you to practice unconditional love by loving the lower and higher Self completely.

Take a deep breath.

Allow this orb of amber/golden light to travel up through the heart pulsating, lodging within the 10th Chakra—the high heart center just above the 8th Chakra. This is your *Sacred Heart Center.* Make a commitment this day to do all you humanly can to spread love and enlightenment out into the world, to others. One of the easiest ways of doing this is to connect frequently with the energy of the Heart Center Love Crystals.

Take a deep breath.

Allow this energy to ascend slowly from the Lower Heart Center — clearing as it transcends the Throat Centre, piercing through to the Third Eye center, through the Crown Center, through the Pyramid of the 8th Chakra, through the Star Triad of the 9th and lodges itself at the top of the 10th Chakra. Floating just above the 8th Chakra you now have an amber/ golden etheric orb of Light which will allow you to work at this particular stage with all that is needed for you to integrate the Spiritual Chakras up to this point and realize the truth of your Angelic/ Universal self.

Take a deep breath.

Bring your attention to the inner silver energy that insulates your etheric membrane, at the fourth-third level of you Aura, as this energy also gives of itself, creating a most beautiful protection and fluidity that manifests as a silver bubble right in the very core of the golden orb.

Take a deep breath.

The golden orb is about 2.5 cm in width and about 9 cm in diameter and floating within its core is a silver bubble of energy small enough to fit into the orb core. Now, gently lower this orb or light until it fits into the top triangle of the 9th Chakra—at the point of the 8 1/2 Chakra. In other words, allow the lower edge of the orb to come to rest on the flat end of the downward pointing triangle that forms part of the star-triad energy within the 9th chakra. In time this will form a support for many other orb energies from the higher charkas to be birthed within your physical being.

Take a deep breath.

Visualize within the very core of the silver energy contained within the amber/golden matrix, a mother of pearl flame about 2.5 cm in height, of an iridescent mother of pearl vibration. You have the *platinum flame* within the iridescent *'mother-of-pearl-like'* vibration at the center of the 9th Chakra and now you have the iridescent *mother of pearl flame* within the silver-amber/ gold or *relating platinum energy* of the 10th Chakra. You are connected to the vibrations and light of the 10th Chakra, and the activation will begin at its own rate in its own way, naturally.

Know that this is only the beginning stage of activating the powerful energy of the Spiritual Chakras within your physical energy field. Few will accept this energy well. Others will find it to be a bit intense; either way, simply relax into it. If you feel uncomfortable drink some water and feel yourself letting go and merging into it.

Take a deep breath.

Relate to these powerful vibrations emitted from the golden sphere and see how the gold, and silver, along with the mother of pearl energies, pulsates light frequencies into the rest of your chakras. First of all begin to visualize these energy orbs of light being transmitted from the 10th

Chakra into the 9th, then 8th then 7th and so forth all the way down into the Root Center. Take your time.

Visualize how the mother of pearl energy increases in vibration now that the amber/golden and silver energies have laid the foundation for this powerful activation by sparking activity within your auric membranes. Allow the mother of pearl energy being emitted by the flame of this center to increase in vibration until your entire energy field vibrates on the frequency of mother of pearl.

Within this powerful transformation of your energy field—claim your authentic angelic Universal Self at one with your human angel. Claim yourself as a Universal light-worker, a planetary grid-keeper, a divine magical-mystical being who lives in miracles, creates in miracles, and expresses only that which is of the most powerful unconditional love.

In so doing, claim yourself as a being who chooses to do, to say, to think and share only that which shall uplift others and to do so by practicing forgiveness of the self, claiming yourself as a most powerful being that trusts your Spiritual Ego to guide you instead of allowing the lower ego to take you off guard. Claim yourself as a wonderful emotional being, a sexual being, an earth being, who claims the creative orb that is alive within you. Remember you are a creative being, a multidimensional being. The differences between you and your immediate family and friends really don't matter. What matters is for you to continue giving of your God-Spark Light to bless them. Allow this higher energy to be integrated within your being, gently. Behind your closed eyes see the *Divine Universal Light* moving within you.

Take a deep breath. OPEN your eyes.

Ground yourself-properly anchoring your energy though your Zero Chakras at the balls of the feet into the earth, making sure you are thoroughly grounded.

Take three deep breaths.

If you feel a swirling or a bit dizzy, stay put, open your eyes and reach upward with your arms. Before leaving, make sure that you are fully back into this NOW space.

END OF MEDITATION — δ

Notes on the 8th Chakra

Notes on The 8th Chakra

V

The Ninth Chakra

In the next stage of your physical body's shifting reality, a realm of many vibrant prismatic colors and dancing energy patterns will emerge. Your body's Chakra System can be viewed as an energy pattern of beautiful colors, circling each of its thirteen major energy centers. Imagine glorious combinations of reds, coral-pinks and vibrant light blues, red-oranges and deep, glowing greens, dancing together in marvelous ways. Picture each energy center working in perfect harmony with each other as one. Let me briefly describe why this is happening to you.

Chakras (your major energy centers) allow your transforming physical body to integrate with its Spiritual body in order to function properly in the new Fifth Dimension Energies. To accomplish these complex intertwining procedures, your Spiritual Hierarchy intends to bring *four additional chakras* online as soon as possible. (The Eighth, Eight and one-half, Ninth and Tenth) These four new centers will permit you to manage the immensity of multi-dimensional information inherent in your new physicality – the physical body walking in harmony and balance with the *Universal body.*

In addition, the four Spiritual Chakras will transform the other seven chakras, known as your *Physical Chakras,* thereby allowing them to take on many new “energetic responsibilities”. Let us now begin to understand this changing life-energy system of your chakras.

9th Chakra: Color: Magenta/Silver

The Ninth Chakra is an interesting chakra. In this chakra, all of the Spiritual abilities lie dormant, waiting to be released and used actively in the outer and inner worlds. This chakra is known as the *Astral Body Ninth Chakra Center* for knowing beyond sight...color is magenta/ silver.

Opening the Ninth Chakra

The Ninth Chakra resides at the back of your head, between the two occipital bones, and is the connection to the Universe. It is outside of time and space and extends through the vastness of space and connects to the Eighth Chakra, through the filter of the Eight and One-Half Chakra, by a luminous cord.

The Ninth Chakra is the *Self—the* Universal Body—that has never been born and will never die. This Self is prior to time, and it never enters the river through which time flows. It is the entire Soul, prior to space, and existed before the Universe manifested. This is the Self that never left the Garden of Eden.

The Ninth Chakra is a very powerful chakra. It is in this chakra that all the super- natural and spiritual abilities lie dormant, waiting to be released and used in the outer and inner worlds. The shift in focus at this time is toward the Divine Universal energy and the accompanying abilities that go along with it. Hence, a great deal of spiritual processing work and Fifth Dimension energy is now being sent into your physical reality to help you open up and expand this energy center. The Ninth Chakra, like the others, has some hard specs to process.

The Ninth Chakra sits behind the head between the two occipital bones at the top of the spine, and spins out to about four feet. It is the first hardwired chakra, and its fluidic twin is the Tenth Chakra. The number of spokes that the Ninth Chakra possesses varies (like in the Eighth Chakra), and its exact number will depend on how open the chakra is. These spokes range in number from ten to twenty thousand. Each spoke is actually a filament or a series of filaments.

When most of these filaments are wired properly and the chakra begins to open, this chakra emits a radiant energy that looks like a spinning rainbow. It depends on what skills an individual is presently pulling out of this skill-storehouse for use in the outer world that will determine the predominate color emanating from this chakra. Assigning a particular color to this chakra tends to be meaningless. The Magenta represents superior strength and knowledge, and the Silver represents the *purification* of the wisdom contained within the Ninth Chakra.

This dynamic chakra holds the *karmic blueprint* of the individual. It stores the skills and abilities learned in all lifetimes. This chakra also holds the key to the Soul's destiny. The Ninth Chakra is the one that connects us to our Third Eye, the Crown Chakra, and back up to the Eighth Chakra by a golden/amber laser light stream going through the brain penetrating the pineal and pituitary glands, out to the Third Eye, causing a Triad of light for illumination and activation of the Universal Body. The evolving human Soul can be broken down into three main types or blueprints: Creator, Healer, Teacher.

Any individual can fit into any one or more of these Soul categories. The predominant category will determine where the Soul is headed after the human-condition is complete. It also will determine the slant of the lifetimes lived, and process any residue for the individual, and then bring forth the kind of skills that are stored in the Ninth Chakra. For example, the Healer Blueprint will be different than the blueprint for the Creator.

The Healer Blueprint will have far more lifetimes spent in some kind of healing capacity, and the skills stored there will reflect and activate this area of expertise.

The Creator Blueprint will have far more lifetimes spent in the creation of things, like artwork, carpentry, organizations, families, etc., and there will be a great number of these kinds of skills stored here for the individual to activate as it begins to spin and open.

Realizing that this chakra can be *one of three types* is important so you avoid the trap of thinking this chakra is not functioning because its energy output seems variable and unstable. There are subtle energy differences with each blueprint, and as you do more healing on this chakra, you will become aware of the energy subtleties of each type. For example, you will find the Teacher Blueprint the most intense, as these people are slated to work directly with the human community. Hence, they tend to have a massive number of lifetimes and skills stored here. Anytime you feel a very powerful and full Ninth Chakra, recognize that this individual has a Teacher Blueprint.

The Creator and Healer Blueprints are much less intense due to the reduced number of lifetimes that are required to be lived for their development. However, keep in mind that this is only generally speaking. The point is not to let the intensity of this chakra fool you into thinking something could be wrong, especially if the first few people you work on are of the Teacher Blueprint.

The Ninth Chakra is the knowledge storage base for the Soul. It houses all the information and life-experiences that are part of that individual Soul. The individual accesses this chakra when he or she brings forth a past-life skill that is presently needed. These previous skills become very important as the individual begins to awaken spiritually and the higher-chakras open. Many of these past lessons and skills must be merged in a kind of synthesis that cements together all of the lessons, both physical and Spiritual, that the Soul has endured. The Soul then learns the true meaning of what was being accomplished from the entire human experience and finally higher spiritual wisdom sets in.

All is well and good with this chakra as long as the past lessons stored here are processed and completed properly. However, what occasionally occurs is that one or two of these lessons are not properly learned or put into perspective, and then the corresponding hardwire connection in this chakra is not complete. When the individual goes to access this particular needed knowledge, it will either be retrieved incompletely or not at all, and they cannot tie together the lessons from those experiences. *Without a proper bond and balance between all influences, the individual will be held back from ascending. Sometimes the ego illusion is the block and must be dissolved by surrender.*

A healing in this chakra may be necessary to properly wire up various aspects of the individual and free them from the limitations imposed by the incorrect wiring. Once the filament is wired properly, the individual will have access to this knowledge and can progress on upward in a free and easy manner.

For example, a person with a Teacher Blueprint will need to bring forth the knowledge of healing at some point, so that they can instruct other healers. If this filament is wired incorrectly due to some past trauma in one of the healing lifetimes, this individual will not be able to access this skill and thereby will be unable to learn the value of healing the self and others. This inability to heal could stop this individual from ascending any further. A simple healing of the Ninth Chakra is all that is needed to free the individual from this limitation. Make note that the specific trauma causing the incorrectly wired filament is immaterial because most likely the trauma has been cleared already. If the trauma has been previously cleared, then *it's the understanding of the lesson* that needs to be clarified and straightened out.

Be careful here. Please understand that the clearing of a trauma does not necessarily wire up the specific skill. The wiring of a skill in the Ninth Chakra occurs naturally when an individual reaches the point where the knowledge of a particular skill turns to wisdom. However, if for some reason the individual is unable to complete the transition of knowledge to wisdom due to some kind of trauma in that lifetime, the filament will not get wired up. The trauma then may be healed in a subsequent lifetime, but in that subsequent lifetime that individual may not be engaged in that particular skill. Basically this can also be an ego/surrender block.

In this example, the trauma gets cleared, but the filament remains incorrectly wired due to the skill not being applied when the wisdom occurred. A healing of this chakra will most certainly fix this problem because all that has to occur is removing the old filament and putting the new filament in its proper place. Then, in a matter of time, the knowledge will be released into the mind of the individual. It is best for the individual to rest a week while meditating daily in order for the filament to begin flowing correctly.

When you heal the Ninth Chakra you will most certainly be in a spiritual trance, taken to a different vibration level yourself, and will see some kind of intricate Soul-circuitry if you have inner vision. The energies will lock you into this chakra and enable you to work with it. Hold one hand over the client's Heart Chakra and the other on the client's Brow Chakra, while reciting a healing or seed sound mantra. Visualize a string of energy going out into the Ninth Chakra from the Heart Center and Third Eye in the form of a triad. When you feel yourself accessing a web of intricate connections, you are there.

Now, try to feel for the connection, either in your mind's eye or by sensing the energy of the pathways, and when you get to the improperly wired filament, feel or see yourself removing the old filament and putting the new filament back to its proper place. Then, check to see if the energy feels or looks right. The correction on the filament will have a silver aura if correct and an orange aura if not complete. Then, if all seems well, return to normal consciousness and withdraw your energy.

The healing of a hardwire chakra is relatively easy once you get the knack of it. You are aided by invisible healers and forces sent to you from Amber by way of the Eight and One-Half Chakra.

These sessions go quickly and do not take a great deal of energy in the process. All you are doing here is replacing and putting into place an energy strand that was not put in properly at birth. There is no balancing or closing that has to get done either. You go in, find the strand, replace it, put it in its place, and leave. Done! Have the client meditate strongly over the next week to ensure and secure the placement.

Personal Issues Associated with the Ninth Chakra

The Ninth Chakra is one of the first levels that vibrate so far beyond human experience that there are no personal issues associated with this chakra.

Shadow Aspects of the Ninth Dimension

Although the filter of the 9th Chakra is protected, the incoming new energy can rarely become so forceful that it vibrates to a powerful, negative energy. Like anything else, you must never violate Spiritual Law as they relate to intergalactic issues.

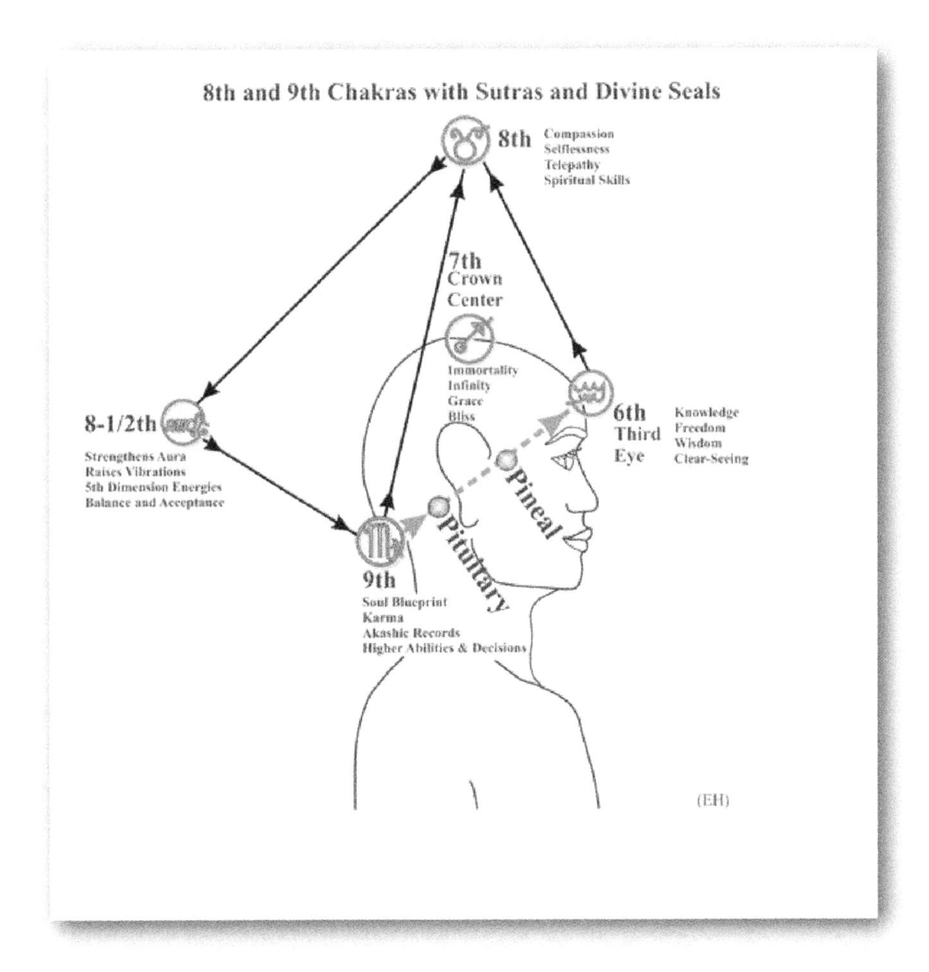

About The Ninth Dimension

- The Ninth dimension primarily focuses its energy on intergalactic activities and endeavors.

- Because the Ninth dimension interconnects galaxies, it has very unusual light frequencies and light/sound harmonics. These light frequencies and harmonics form a self-regulating system that oversees the evolution and harmony of all of the galaxies. This is a very important function as no one galaxy can evolve at a rate or pace to imbalance the Universe.

- Barbara Hand Clow in her book, *Alchemy of Nine Dimensions,* writes with great clarity about the Ninth Dimension. She maintains that the Milky Way is the entirety of the Ninth Dimension and contains a black hole in its very middle from which flow intergalactic energies. She feels that from this source are derived the origins of time itself.

- Adrian Gilbert, author of *The Mayan Prophecies*, says that the Mayan *Universal Tree of Life* that governs the evolutionary cycles of this planet, vibrates to the Ninth Dimension.

- From the perspective of human Soul evolution, once you have vibrated to all nine dimensions, you have officially completed your Universal soul experience and are free to come or leave the Universe, at will.

- When I want to safely travel in various worlds, I like to enter from the Ninth Dimension because border guards, such as the Council of Nine, watch out for my welfare and recalibrate my energetic field vibration. Intergalactic realms are the inner spiritual planes for many cultures on the earth, so traveling here is like sliding between the culture and their respective spiritual worlds. I have been Soul traveling since birth.

- The Ninth is the dimension of *quarks.* Quarks are truly quantum in their reality. The quark aspect of us allows our multidimensionality. Quarks seemingly appear and disappear very quickly. When they appear in this vibrational reality, they support our Third Dimensional reality. When they disappear to another dimension, world, or galaxy, they support that aspect of our Soul expression. This instantaneous presence between and among the other dimensions, realms and galaxies allows us to continually be in contact and communication with our other parts, or parallel lives.

Opening the Spiritual Chakras is the beginning of non-duality between the dimensions. It is not the simultaneous consciousness of all of our multidimensionality such as at the Tenth and Eleventh Dimensions, but it is the beginning of non-duality in a very real way, on the physical level. The Oneness consciousness begins and there is absolutely no thought or feeling of separation.

Traveling in the Ninth Dimension

At a time when I Soul traveled in this dimension often, I primarily spent time working with inner planes councils such as the *Council of Nine.* This Council regulates the comings and goings of Souls and entities onto the planet and into the galaxy with exit and entrance visas. They are in essence high-level governance for the intergalactic negotiations; this council also deals with high-level violations of Spiritual Law.

- I have spent time traveling in this dimension in my Universal body, surfing the harmonics within their intricate complexity.
- When working with clients and supporting their Spiritual development by overseeing Spiritual initiations, you will work from and within this level.
- One works from this dimension whenever working with transition a Soul from this life to the next.

Associated Sensations when Traveling Here

Contrasted with the coarse strength of the Eighth dimensional energies, the Ninth Dimension energies are smooth and subtle. The harmonics allow for a most relaxing, yet totally absorbing experience. *Subtle refinement* would be the best phrase for this experience. This is why many of you vibrate well with Richard Shulman's *Ascension Harmonics* because his music vibrates to the Ninth Dimension energies. (www.richheartmusic.com)

Application of Ninth Dimensional Energies

- Dimensional energies from here can be transferred or downloaded by healers to their clients to stimulate the brain to send messages to the body for healing.
- This is the dimensional level needed to access permission to work with Soul evolutionary beings.
- This is the dimensional level used to inform cells to shift their vibration and dimensional levels; they are called the Re-creation codes.
- I love to work in and from the Ninth Dimension with clients. When I peer inside the atom and work with the quark awareness in the body, I see its inner planes which look like threads with seven levels to them. (See: *Ascension—Accessing The Fifth Dimension*) This quark level helps the pure essence of Self to enter the body and anchor it, thus truly spiritualizing matter. As I work to activate and awaken this level in my client, they tend to respond with "in the body" feelings of joy and exhilaration. They also report feeling more solid and "more themselves" than ever before. It is truly an "in the body/out of the body" feeling. That's one of the hallmarks of evolutionary work, and gives the healer a full sense of gratitude to the Divine. Deep work in the brain is often done from and with this dimension, and its energies guide and council at this level and love to work with evolution at all levels.

Ninth Dimension Guides

- Council of Nine
- Amber and more advanced Angels
- Some Master Yogi's and teachers off and on the Planet
- Energies of the Keys of Enoch

Sutras that Convey the Vibration of the Ninth Dimension
Acceptance, balance, integration as well as evolution, raises vibration, strengthens aura, intergalactic, Spiritual refinement, inner planes initiations, allurement represents security, reliability, intelligence, stability, modesty, maturity, conservation, old age, sadness, and boredom.

The Ninth Chakra color (Magenta/Silver) relates to the seat of the Ecological Self and is associated with the sense of complexity. The overall theme for this level is Universal intelligence and integration.

The Eighth, Eight and one-half, and Ninth Chakras are unconventional and together could comprise what might be considered another Chakra—an energy without a center that spreads across the galaxies from the beginning of time and space into an unending future.

The Ninth Chakra is where you meet and work with your *Universal Body*—the etheric or Light Body. One might refer to this level as the seat of the *Whole Self* and associated with the sense of awe and union. The overall theme would certainly be *an unknowing mystery.*

What does being fully conscious mean? It means three things:

1. You become multi-dimensional in your conscious thinking, in your reality, and in your capabilities;

2. Your physical body amalgamates with all other aspects of your new reality;

3. You change your energy systems entirely. In this way, your physical system actually integrates with your multi-dimensionality as well as your physical, mental, emotional, and Spiritual bodies.

Universal/Light Body Development

Universal light body developing methods—two-stranded DNA helix human beings transmuting into TWELVE helix strand human beings with light body. The Spiritual Intensives access this twelve-strand helix, which is the strongest helix known to this Universe.

Changing a current two-helix DNA person into a twelve-helix DNA person is a *one to two year program, to be completed on a massive scale worldwide.* Because, as you may know: what a two-helix DNA persons' conscious mind and body can't hold—the *two-helix DNA persons' sub-conscious mind and body can.* If whatever the two-helix persons' sub-conscious mind and body can't hold, then their *super-conscious mind and body can* and on upward. Whatever your *super conscious mind and body* can't hold, your *collective conscious can* and so on. However, the Soul's higher dimensions will experience all this knowledge continually. Third Dimension beings are always half-conscious due to their limited two-helix DNA. They can't hold such information and resonate with that experience on a fully multidimensional conscious level.

This is what a two helix DNA person has to deal with every day. That is why we call the two-helix DNA person half-conscious, where sometimes it knows everything and sometimes it doesn't. Just like sometimes you remember and sometimes don't. Or sometimes awake in spirit, and sometime asleep in spirit and so forth.

For a Twelve helix DNA person—there is no experience of limitation or disconnection. Their experience is whatever the collective mind knows as well as what the conscious mind knows and experiences. What the conscious mind knows and experiences, and whatever the subconscious mind knows and experiences, the super-conscious mind knows also.

The key to get to the Twelve helix DNA body (Universal/light body type) is that you have to understand and connect with the important relationship of the Thymus Gland and the Hyper Thymus Gland, as well as soma light body hormone to the Universal light body development.

A two-helix person cannot understand a lot of multidimensional energy and information simultaneously on a continuous basis all the time. In order for a two-helix DNA person to become a twelve-helix DNA person or Universal body, the healer must understand the relation of the Thymus and Hyper Thymus to the soma hormone as well as Universal/light body development.

Remember the Thymus Gland's location inside the body, in the upper chest, but below the throat known also as the *higher heart,* is between your Fifth and Four Chakra in a two DNA helix human body structure. By accessing the 10th chakra it produces a hormone and *creates an advanced immune system* for the body and mind. As for the Hyper Thymus gland, its physical location is in the center of your brain.

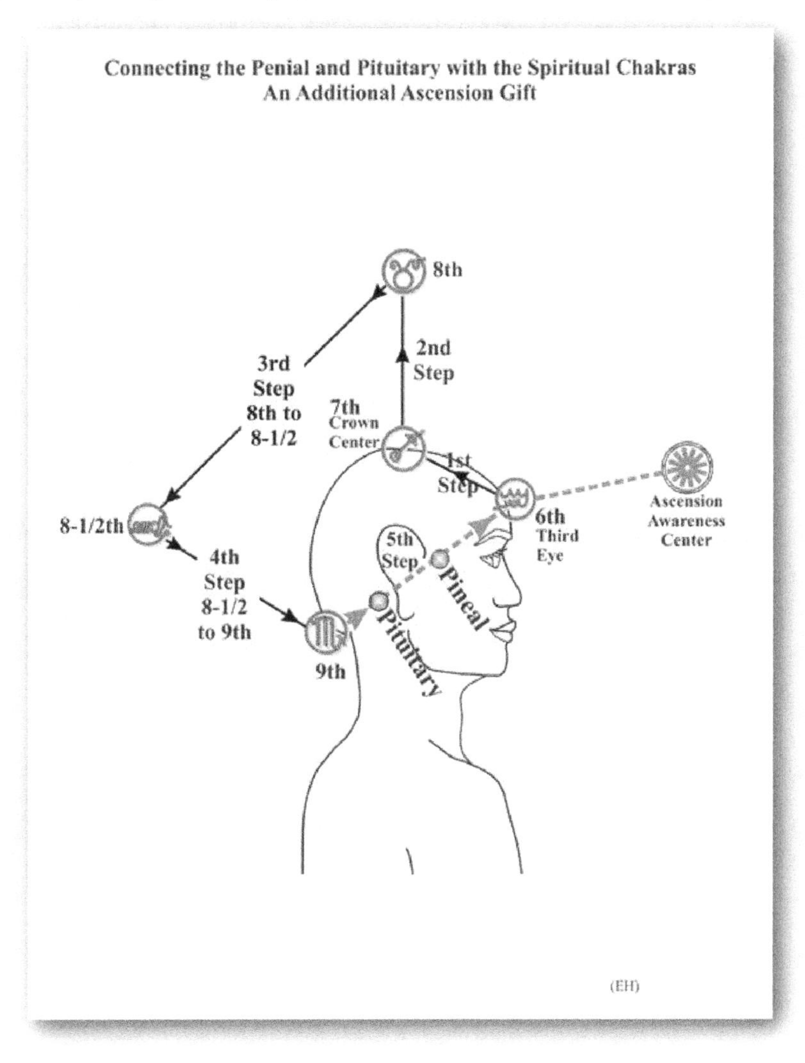

A Stronger Third Eye—The New Point Of Healing Power

The Hyper Thymus gland has a relationship or is connected to the top part of the Pineal Gland and the bottom part of the Pituitary Gland. They produce soma, a divine hormone or Universal body hormone which has the power to transmute the two-helix DNA strands into the twelve-helix DNA strands. This is the DNA activation process. The hormone that is needed is called soma or the Universal body hormone and in order to produce this Universal body hormone (soma for transmutation of the two-helix DNA strand into a twelve-helix DNA strands) you must meditate on these two points of focus, the Thymus Gland and the Hyper Thymus Gland to give a harmonious energy flow.

Once the connection is made between the Ninth and Sixth Chakras, and the Ninth Chakra is spinning properly, there is an additional Spiritual gift—that of Clairvision. Your inner vision messages ability will expand, as well as past-life recall. Your intuitive sensitivity will expand and grow as well as the experience of deeper meditations.

Universal Body Meditation

First Step

The first area to focus on is the Thymus Gland area by visualizing a purple *blue/silver light*: like a candle flame on the upper chest below the throat area and above the heart chakra area in the center of your body. The purple blue flame should be visualized right there, about the size of a candle flame. Meditate on this area for ten to twenty minutes. Then for ten minutes, you should expand the purple blue/silver flame through your aura—using your imagery and extending this energy out about twelve feet around you, engulfing everything. During this stage you will feel warmth in that area as well as a powerful energy surge. In the last ten minutes visualize an amber light flowing down from the 10th chakra, the Universal Body's heart center. *You must practice thirty minutes every day to begin to open/spin the Ninth Chakra.* This takes focus, dedication, action, and application.

Second Step

The second step is to focus at the point or area between the eyebrows, the Third Eye or Sixth Chakra. This chakra is related to the hyper thymus gland; therefore visualize a little golden light there, the size of your thumb, for ten minutes.

Third Step

The third area to visualize is in the center of your brain or head. Just visualize a golden sun there and the size of that golden sun is the size of a ping-pong ball. Do this for ten minutes. Afterward, visualize the golden sun growing to the full size of your head, filling it and shining outwards for another ten minutes. Then visualize this golden energy as a golden water spout, springing right out from your head through the Crown Chakra, reaching up to the Eighth Chakra, and then the Tenth, like water from a fountain. Continue through the Eighth Chakra and go up in the air about twenty feet and then, with your mind's eye again seeing the golden water coming back down and hitting the Eight and one-half chakra, see an Amber glow filtering into the Ninth Chakra and coming into the back side of the Pineal Gland.

You have created a double helix channel—or golden triad. (See: pg. 136) Allow this new energy, the filtered Fifth Dimension energy, to soak your whole body, clothing, aura, inner organs, skin, etc. In this golden energy of Amber Light, you will create the Universal/light body and bring back or activate your two- helix DNA strand into a twelve-helix DNA, Universal body type, and all of your seventy-two psychic channels or chakras, both major and minor, will be open and fully developed.

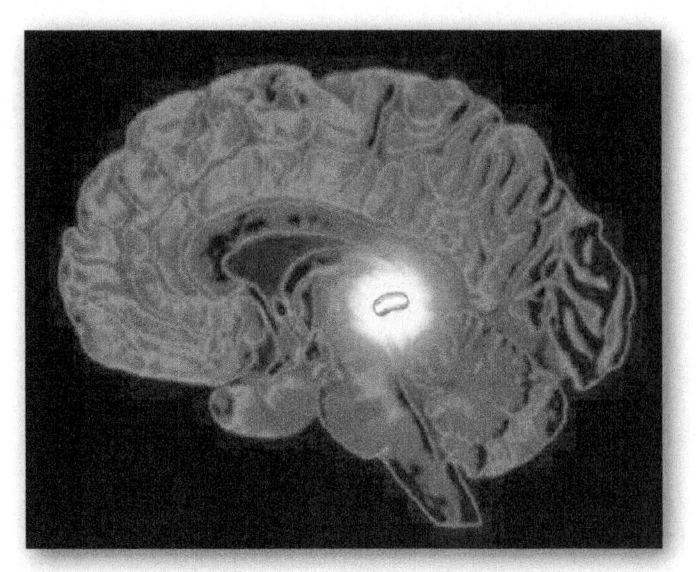

THE PINAL GLAND IN THE BRAIN

The Third Eye Triad

Opening of the Third Eye

Dark Gray Triad - Thinking - Talking - Action

Light Gray Triad - Love - Peace Harmony

White Triad - 5th Dimension: Ascension - Telepathy - Soul Travel

The Fifth Dimension brings a new energy with it, expanding the Third Eye vibration and capabilities. You will be able to send out distant healing energies with this new, white, and clear Triad as well as texting others through telepathic messages and Soul travel with your Etheric Body.

(EH)

Fourth Step

The fourth step is that of Amber—the Angel of Light: focus on the core star-gate point at the center of the body between the Second and Third Chakras on the physical body—visualize a bright White Light at your Solar Plexus center, and feel at one with the world around you and the cosmos.

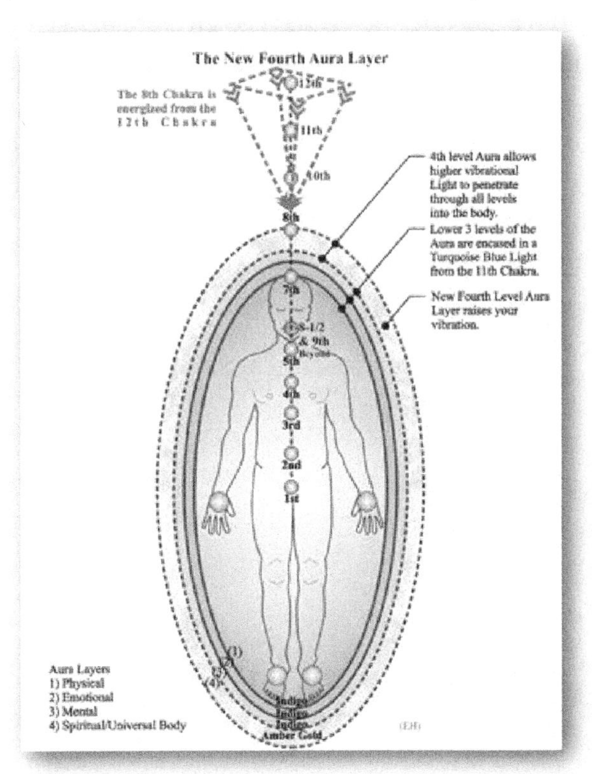

The New Fourth Level of the Aura

This diagram shows our Spiritual Energy System as well as the new fourth level to the Aura. This new level is designed to hold and filter the Light energy from the Double Helix as we begin to access its Light and vibration for Ascension.

There are also systems for energetic balancing that work with your photograph and help keep your energies open to receiving the higher Light, without subconscious resistances. One system is known as the *AIM Program* with

Stephen Lewis. Stephen says. *"Hereditary imbalances are the substance basically that forms you. And you have a lifetime to deal with them or have them deal with you."* The AIM Program states; You, your consciousness, emotions, illnesses – *everything* – is energy, and everything has a unique frequency. When the body's energetic frequencies are in harmony, there are no blockages to the flow of Life Force. The greater your flow of Life Force, the greater your personal power to create, to heal, to reach your potential.

As you begin to understand how you create energetic imbalances, you gain insight into your innate ability to heal yourself, and gain a greater understanding that it is your responsibility to do so.
(www.aim2livewell.info)

Amber—Our Fifth Dimension Guardian Angel Overshadows Us

Fifth Step

Now feel the Angel, Amber, blowing the Golden Light into your Ninth Chakra— flowing down to your core star-gate and visualize the core star-gate spinning at your Solar Plexus center and see that light energy spreading out through the physical body and blending with every atom, cell, and particle of your physical existence and feel that light energy moving out into the ***four auric layers*** of your existence. You will begin to feel *at One* with all things living on the planet. The healer can help facilitate this process during the healing session.

Remember

The secret here is to practice, practice, practice. You will have many psychic side effects from this method, and may experience levitation, seeing auras, telepathic communication—your hair will turn white or different colors. You will experience many multidimensional travels, like teleportation and harmony with the earth, swim in the water at one with the fish, or walk through any solid object. It will become normal when using this method, as well as creating a strong internal psychic vision. This is a new Fifth Dimensional healing method for incorporating many different sixth-sense gifts at once. You will become gods and goddess using this method of psychic development.

Notes on The 9th Chakra

VI

The Tenth Chakra

The Tenth Chakra is the *Spiritual heart center* chakra. When the Tenth Chakra starts to open, the individual will begin to manifest many of the skills they have learned in all of their previous lives, especially emotional growth. These individuals will seem to excel at anything they undertake, and any project they are involved with will take off from their influence.

It is not that they are just good at doing everything; rather they are tapping into previous skills learned in past lives. The barriers between the past selves are breaking down and knowledge and wisdom begins to flow through time and space.

Typically this chakra is responsible for Divine Creativity, new ideas, synchronicity of life, the merging of the masculine and feminine within. How do these emerging skills relate to these qualities? Well it is these emerging skills and the taping of previous lives that make all these elements come about. *Divine creativity is the ability to create all facets of your life in perfect harmony.* When this harmony starts to manifest, the individual's life just clicks. It will seem as if this person is always in the right place at the right time. Divine energy flows out of this chakra and into the physical part of the individual and brings perfection into everything he or she does. Tapping into past lives does not discriminate between male or female lifetimes, allowing the individual to begin to merge and balance the masculine and feminine within themselves. This merging brings even more harmony into a person's life because they are not prone to either the masculine or feminine energy or the faults that each of those polarities tends to bring up. A gender balance exists within the individual. We all have a masculine and feminine energy source, and the individual is free to tap into the best that each energetic polarity has to offer.

These individuals will not seem overly masculine or feminine in nature; they will be neutral in qualities, from an outside perspective. Of course, it can take years for this kind of transformation to occur in an individual, after that person's Tenth Chakra starts to open up. They will not wake up one day and be neutral. The individual has to let go of the previous polarity they were prone toward and begin to embrace the new neutral energies within them. Keep this in mind when working on a client and you sense that the Tenth Chakra is starting to open. You may want to advise them that gentle changes in either their masculine or feminine side may begin to occur over the next several years and there is nothing to worry about, it is quite normal.

Also, this masculine and feminine neutralizing has little to do with sexual predisposition. Nor should there be any change in the sexual alignment in that person's life. You are not going to be attracted to men now if you were attracted to women before. However the individual may find it easier to relate to the other sex as the masculine and feminine merge within them.

Now, what sort of challenges/problems are you apt to find with this chakra? Well for one, many Ninth Chakra challenges will show up when the Tenth Chakra starts to open. *Remember! The odd number chakras contain the skills that are used in the following even numbered.* For this reason you most likely will not begin to do any healing on the Ninth Chakra till the Tenth starts to awaken and spin within you. It is when the individual tries to use these past life skills contained in the Ninth Chakra that the Tenth Chakra challenges begin. The filaments in the Ninth Chakra may not be wired properly so when the individual tries to access a past life skill, they have great difficulty. At this point you would need to go in and do a healing on the Ninth Chakra and then the skills contained in the Tenth Chakra would develop normally over a period of time in that person's life.

For example, let's say a person with an opening Tenth Chakra has a deep urge to take up writing. They try to develop this skill but it comes very slowly and with much frustration. Other aspects of this person's life are developing normally; except when they try to acquire this skill it is not as forthcoming as the others. In this case, a Ninth Chakra challenge/blockage exists and a healing in that chakra will be necessary. However, if the person was able to grasp the skill quite easily, but was unable to use that skill in harmony, then a Tenth Chakra problem exists.

It is the Tenth Chakra that is responsible for integrating the skill into the person's daily life. If that skill is there but presents an integration problem in that person's life, creating disharmony in some way, then some aspect of the Tenth Chakra is not functioning properly. Most likely there are energy blocks in this chakra and so the synchronicity of life is not fully developed. Fear is the emotion that can block a Tenth Chakra. Some remaining fear associated with a skill from a past life remains in the energy field. You may have to do a past life healing to remove the last of this fear and bring the Tenth Chakra to full functioning. If you have good inner sight, these blocks may show up as small disturbances that seem to float over the spinning chakra. These energy disturbances cause the energetic flow to slow down the swirling outward effect that this chakra has on the entire being.

The Tenth Chakra can be seen like a tornado of light filling the individual with perfect Divine energy. A fully functional Tenth Chakra will have a rainbow-like effect coming from its swirling mass of energy. If any blockages are present, these disturbances of blocked energy will cause the rainbow effect to be broken up. The individual is not fully bathed in the integration energies of the Tenth Chakra.

The Tenth Chakra is a brilliant amber/yellow and is most like the Heart Charka in the lower chakra system, the Fourth Chakra Center. The 4th center Heart Chakra takes all the energy from the other chakras and processes it so it can be used physically. The Tenth Chakra takes all the energy from all the other Spiritual Chakras and transforms it so the individual can use the energies from the Spiritual Chakras in harmony with one's life. For this reason, any kind of spiritual disharmony that may exist in a spiritually awakened individual can most likely be caused by blockages in the Tenth Chakra. For example, the inability to integrate the masculine and feminine currents, inability to use an advanced spiritual skill properly, fear of acquiring some skill that is currently needed, unable to get along with others or accept others, especially those that are Spiritually awakened, feeling threatened by certain advanced nonphysical skills like out-of-body travel.

Please note that even though we have not talked about advanced spiritual skill development, which is covered in the Eleventh Chakra, it is the Tenth Chakra's job to integrate those skills into the individual in a harmonious manner. Any difficulty with advanced spiritual skills that are developing would fall into a 10th Chakra challenge. The individual may have some fear, blockage or inability when applying these new skills.

Healing the Tenth Chakra involves removing the blockages that may be here and lifting any fear that may reside, as well. Universal Light, is especially useful with this chakra. Hold a very intense **turquoise blue light** in your mind as you work on this chakra. This light will soothe and remove all the rough spots creating a calming effect on the individual. You can use a mantra and the Circle of Light to help unlock the balancing effect of the masculine and feminine. Example: om shreem reem kleem

The Tenth Chakra is located ten to twelve feet from the top of the Crown Chakra, just outside the fourth Auric field of energy, so you can't really access it like a normal chakra. This chakra is outside of the body and aura field. Position yourself over the Heart Chakra of the client, and imagine your nonphysical hands extending through this chakra and up to the Tenth Chakra. Then send the healing energy into the Tenth Chakra as a laser of amber/gold light, while holding on to the inner vision of the energy going through the lower Heart Chakra into the Tenth Chakra. Energy follows intent, and the Heart Chakra is the lower physical center to the Tenth Chakra's higher center, so it makes an easy place to access this higher spiritual energy.

If you use crystals in your healing work, dousing a Heart Chakra with the intent of dousing the Tenth Chakra will not work. You will just douse the Heart Chakra. You have to construct a *crystal transformer* to send the Universal Turquoise Blue Light energy up to the Tenth Chakra. Take three small, six-sided crystals and place in a circle around the Heart Chakra. Then take your main crystal and hover it over the center of the crystal circle, the vortex or power point, sending an Amber/Golden Light through the main crystal. With this method, your client may think you have lost your mind, but this method should allow you to read and work on the Tenth Chakra using a Fifth Dimension accessing crystal.

Keep in mind that the Tenth Chakra is the Heart Chakra of the Spiritual Chakra System. If you find faults or blocked up energy here, the entire Spiritual Chakra spin harmony will suffer. If you see lots of small energy problems within the Eighth, Ninth, Eleventh and Twelfth Chakras, suspect an energy conversion problem with the Tenth Chakra. Use the turquoise blue light or perhaps some crystals, working through the Heart Chakra, to heal and balance this chakra. Also it would be a good idea to see this client four to six weeks later to check to see if any other healing work needs to be done in this chakra. The Tenth Chakra has layers to it. You heal one and the next one will come up several weeks later for healing. Once all the layers are healed you will most likely not need to see the client for a long time.

The human mean is forty-four. Continue the follow-up visits until the client comes in with a clear Tenth Chakra. At that time, it is ethically out of order to ask for any kind of appointment payment. Your payment will come in other ways. You have just helped another Ascend, and that must be your focus.

The 10th, 11th, and 12th Chakras are at the levels of energy that support transformation and bring a Universal harmony and balance down to the lower charkas. Let me explain that there are many levels, but we have only shared a few here. Instead of confusing you, just know that this is complex energy you are working with, and the overruling energy that facilitates this action is found within the complexity of the 9th Chakra.

To Review

The 9th Chakra fits into the dynamics of the 8th Chakra because of the Arcturian Angel, Amber, and the filtering of these energies, which then share a communication creating harmonious dynamics with the Crown Centre. Therefore the whole system eventually works as one harmonious unit, yet serves as individual links of your sacred chain of consciousness. One link feeds the other and so the next feeds into the one to follow. Within the 9th Chakra you are exposed to extreme high vibrations as with the remainder of the Sacred Chakras up to the Thirteenth Energy Level Center, which serves as an overruling chamber of Light for the upper and lower chakras.

As each Chakra opens, you are taken into a whole new vibration, an increased frequency level, because in the 9th Chakra you have your grounding to *a higher homing filter* which connects to the 8th chakra and creates your physical Soul connection to the higher Divine Masters at the Twelfth Dimension Level.

In the 9th Chakra you have your connection to the magnetosphere energy, the gravity, as well as the crystalline grids (the traverse lines), which remind you of your connection to the planet as a grid keeper and *Universal Light Worker*. This serves by anchoring the energy. Here at the level of the 10th Chakra you now need to relate to the invisible forces and other energies in its Angelic form to support this transformation.

Within the higher Chakra Centers the objective is more about energy than matter. Within the lower energy centers you worked with matter and its effects on the various centers, especially within the lower aspects of these energies. In the higher centers, the aim is to shift energy more than matter, so it becomes energy or frequency rather than factual matter. Because it is an all- powerful new energy, many won't be able to integrate it as yet, but believe me over time these chakras will begin to open. They have to if you want to continue on walking this planet in the energies of Ascension. It is like anything else in life, the more you connect to it, practice it, use it, and more specifically invoke it, the more powerful it becomes.

Notes on The 10th Chakra

VI

The Eleventh Chakra

The Egyptians knew that solar systems are almost insignificant compared to galaxies. They explored the Eleventh Chakra, which is the Galactic Chakra. Every galaxy has an organization to it. From visual inspection, the Egyptians knew that our galaxy contained more star systems than we can precisely count. There are tens of billions of them. Consciousness must expand outward to broader horizons, to travel about the Milky Way, and consider it as a single large cultural entity. Yet even this is still local in a sense, and not the end of the story of this vast Universe. Somehow, the Egyptians knew there was something more. There are light sources outside the range of our galaxy just as there are countries outside the range of Egypt. They could see many stars that lie outside the Milky Way, and might well have imagined that there are far distant Milky Ways. What if these points of Light are galaxies rather than stars, and what if there are as many or more galaxies as there are stars in a galaxy?

The Eleventh Chakra —Deep Aqua Blue/Silver

Typically, it can take any number of years for this Spiritual Chakra to completely open. The Eleventh and the Twelfth Chakras take the longest time to fully blossom. It can take one to seven years for the Eighth through Tenth Chakras to open and another additional one to five years for the Eleventh Chakra to open. The Twelfth Chakra is the last chakra to open, and it will not start opening until the Eleventh is well on its way. How long the Spiritual Chakras actually take to open really depends on the individual and the rate at which that individual is evolving.

Please note that this timeframe is just an approximation of how long it *could* take. It does not mean your chakras will take this long to open. It just means that the Spiritual Chakras do take time to come to a fully functional state. In my own case, my Spiritual Chakras started opening at birth. Only in the last ten years has my 12th Chakra opened to what is a fully functional state. The Spiritual Chakras, Eight to Ten, opened within the first fifteen years of life and the Eleventh opened at age thirty-six.

It is not my intention to limit or impose any kind of framework on the individual. But I do not want to sugar coat the spiritualization process. You are a physical creature evolving in a spiritual system and that system uses time to forge knowledge into wisdom. Some things have to happen before other things, and usually it takes time for that to occur. As you can see, my own progress was not the speedy way, and I think it is the more typical way. My reference to how long it takes for these chakras to open is based on my own personal experience with myself and with my students over the years. I certainly have had exceptions to the rule along the way.

Your spiritual journey is yours and it is unique. So anything is possible and certainly the Spiritual Chakras can open fully within a very short period of time in these new Fifth Dimension energies if it is appropriate for you. There just cannot be any ego race with this Divine process.

The Eleventh Chakra contains the energetic connections necessary so the individual can manifest advanced Spiritual skills and travel beyond the limits of time and space, teleportation, bi-location, telekinesis, and instantaneous manifestation of thoughts into matter. Keep in mind that while this chakra possesses these skills, the individual will not actually start to manifest or master these skills until the Twelfth Chakra starts to open.

The reason for this advanced skill development is not to possesses some neat tricks. No, the reason these skills exist is to help prepare the individual for the next phase of his or her existence after Ascension. The Eleventh Chakra contains the path of the Soul in its new form without the restrictions of matter, time and space. It is a glimpse of the individual in its Ascended Universal life form while still retaining much physical matter. At this stage in the development, the individual has merged with the Soul, the *mother* aspect of divinity, and will soon merge with the Monad, the father aspect of divinity. The soul (small s) is often referred to as the individual's core self without a physical body. The Soul (capital S) is the part of the Self that has learned all the physical lessons and has become self-realized. The Eleventh Chakra is referred to as the *mother aspect of divinity.* The individual merges with the Soul at some point during the opening of the 8th to 10th Chakras.

The next step is the merger with the Monad, *a symbol used by ancient Greek philosophers, including Plato, Pythagoras, and Aristotle, to describe God or the totality of all beings. Metaphysical and theological theory describes "monism" as the concept of "one essence"* and it begins when the 11th and 12th charkas begins to open. Complete merging with the Monadic level of divinity results in Ascension and the annihilation of the physical body and replacement of the Universal Light body.

When the Eleventh Chakra starts to open, the individual will become aware of the larger picture of his or her multidimensional self, that his or her existence in physical reality limitations is just one manifestation of many simultaneous existences on other planes of existence. This explanation gives a hint to what awaits the individual after *Ascension: the working toward becoming conscious on all planes of existence, not just the physical one.* (ej)

When this awakening to the larger Self begins, the individual may get glimpses of his experience in these other dimensions. It can be a bit confusing to the individual if they are unaware of what is happening. For a time they may think they are losing their grip on reality. However these sporadic experiences into larger dimensions are normal at this stage of development. The *Monad* is waking up in the physical self and starting to introduce the individual gradually into the *Universal Body* and what awaits him or her.

As a result of this expansion in consciousness, many healing sessions on this chakra will deal with helping the individual cope with the changes in experiences beyond the physical. It's important that this chakra open in a gradual and even manner, or the individual could be thrust into what seems like a chaotic existence. Gentle rose light or rose quartz can help here to soften the opening of this chakra. Normally the opening and integration of this chakra should go fine, but some individuals have a habit of pushing themselves hard throughout their evolutionary process. Again, this is a warning about the Ego.

So when they come to this stage in their development, it seems like nothing is happening. They respond by pushing even harder, when in fact a great deal is occurring subtly. This reason is why the rose quartz Light to the Eleventh Chakra can help greatly. It introduces the energy of self-love and that everything is as it should be. It allows the individual to *trust what is happening and go with the flow of it.* Most of this unrest occurs in the first year or so that this chakra opens. After that period the individual will grow more accustomed to the changes.

Working on the Eleventh Chakra takes some higher knowledge and can be tricky. Similar to healing the Tenth Chakra, you have to reach the energy by working through the lower chakras. The Eleventh Chakra is located fifteen feet over the head of the individual. Place one hand on the Heart Chakra and the other hand on the Solar Plexus. Imagine and feel your golden/amber laser light leaving from the center of your hand, moving upward though the individual to the Eleventh Chakra. Let the rose light flow from your rose quartz crystal into the center of the Eleventh Chakra. In fact you should always start and finish a healing on this chakra with this rose quartz light.

If you want to place the crystal field around the Heart Chakra, as you did for the Tenth Chakra, you can do this as well to help empower the Light movement up into the higher Spiritual Chakra. Rose quartz would really do well as your power crystal that you are holding at the Heart Chakra, but clear quartz can also be used.

Typical Eleventh Chakra problems, besides the one mentioned earlier, will deal with the implementation of advanced Spiritual skills. Keep in mind that these skills won't strongly manifest till the Twelfth Chakra starts to open, but once it does, you will have to go in and try to rewire the particular skill that seems to be erratic. This rewiring technique is very similar to what was explained on the Ninth and Tenth Chakras. Vibrate your Light silently till you start to see the inner circuitry with your inner sight or your hands start to move, and are invisibly directed in making the connections.

When you feel the healing is finished then seal the chakra with rose quartz Light. Tell the client to drink lots of water and take it easy for the next few weeks as the rewiring work settles into the person's energy field. No apparent results may be immediately seen. Typically a healing on the Eleventh Chakra will take one to four weeks to affect the individual on a physical level, and then a balance and improvement will be seen over time. If necessary you can repeat an Eleventh Chakra healing, but no sooner than six to eight weeks from the previous healing. Because of the intensity and distance of the Eleventh Chakra, a repeat healing is often timely and necessary.

The Eleventh Chakra is the Spiritual Library of the individual. In that library are the total contents needed to operate as a human and a *Divine Universal being.* Sometimes the contents have to be organized, put into order, or some housekeeping done. Think of your work on this chakra like a librarian in a library; you are there to put things in order but not to change anything you find.

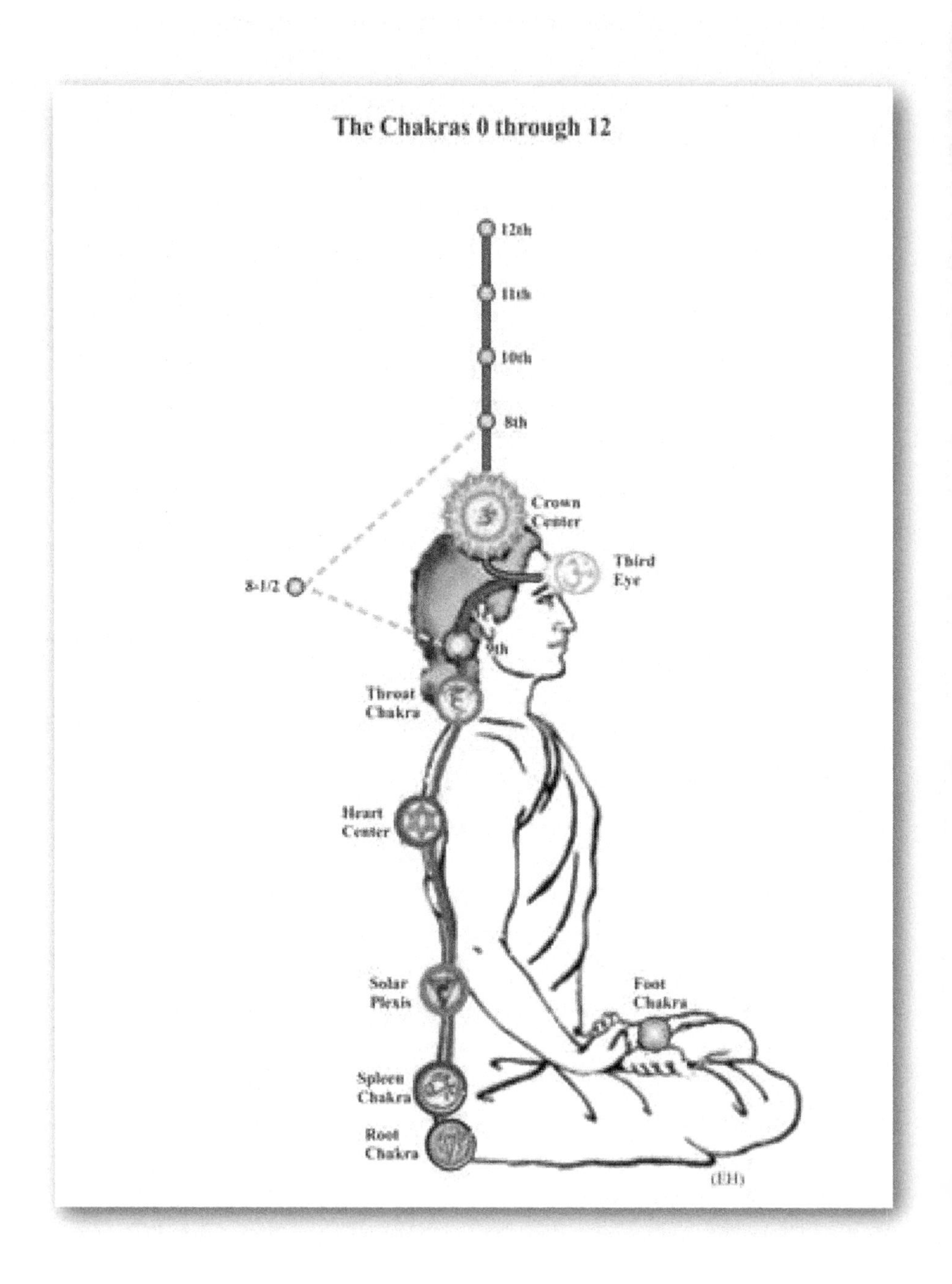
The Chakras 0 through 12
12th
11th
10th
8th
Crown
Center
Third
Eye
8-1/2
Throat
Chakra
Heart
Center
Solar
Plexis
Foot
Chakra
Spleen
Chakra
Root
Chakra
(EH)

Notes on The 11th Chakra

Notes on The 11th Chakra

VIII

The Twelfth Chakra

The 12th Chakra, what a brilliant and wonderful sight this chakra is to see with the Third Eye! It vibrates like a swirling color-filled sun that can only be truly appreciated in out-of-body states or with the mind's inner eyes. The 12th Chakra is a reflection of the Universal Being, individualized. It burns brightly and is hot because a sun provides warmth, light, and energy. Thus the 12th Chakra is the source of the individual's strength and power and ability to create change not only in the physical dimension, but the nonphysical dimensions as well. The symbol for the 12th chakra is the sign of infinity.

The 12th Chakra contains the Ascension energies, designed from the Universal Creator, which are used at the proper time to bathe all the chakras below it in Ascension energy and cause them to accelerate faster than light. The Twelfth Dimension was the original First Dimension, because it was the first one created within this Universe. This Twelfth Chakra energy eventually results in the annihilation of the physical body and the manifestation of the Universal Body, or Light body, in its place. At this point, when this chakra is open, the individual Soul is fully Ascended and can go anyplace in the Universe.

The Root Chakra is a cousin to the Twelfth Chakra because the Root Chakra contains the *kundilini energy, which is seed energy from the 12th chakra,* placed there to accelerate the individual to the first stage of Spiritual enlightenment. The second stage is the release of the Ascension energies contained in the 12th Chakra, released downward through the other dimensions and Spiritual Chakras, to propel the individual into a new existence beyond time and space, as well as the Fifth Dimension.

The 12th Chakra has 777,777 spokes. It rotates at 768,167 rotations per minute. The 12th Chakra is masculine and the 11th Chakra is feminine. By masculine and feminine we do not mean in human terms. Masculine current is creative, outgoing, vibrant, and forceful. Feminine current is loving, inner, nurturing, and subtle.

The 11th Chakra contains the advanced skills and the 12th releases the energy to manifest these skills such as: out-of-body experiences outside the solar system and out-of-body time travel beyond 200 years; healing of self and others, sometimes instantaneous, or at the very least, rapid spontaneous healing. Telekinesis and teleportation are also possible but these two do not show themselves until just prior to the Ascension energies completing its pre-ascension process. Control over the natural elements can also be developed, like air, water, fire, earth, to an advanced degree when the Twelfth Chakra begins opening.

The 12th Chakra is the doorway to the home of the Masters, cosmos, and beyond. For this reason, many of the skills released here are to be used *off the earth within the outer realms of the Solar System.* Any sort of problems associated with these advanced skills can be caused by an incorrectly wired 11th Chakra, but realizing or even coming across people with problems here will be very slim.

Not many healers are apt to get a visit from someone saying they are having trouble traveling back to the birth of the Universe, please have a look at my 11th and 12th Chakras. What you are likely to see are blocked Ascension energies in the lower Spiritual charkas within this chakra.

Blocked ascension energies can cause very strange problems, like spontaneous, uncontrolled, out-of-body adventures, uncontrolled spontaneous movements of physical objects, the appearing and disappearing of objects, uncontrolled healing ability, uncontrolled inner visions that disrupt the normal flow of the day. What happens is this blocked energy backs up, and when it gets strong enough it bursts through and over-energizes the 11th Chakra, releasing these skills abruptly and unintentionally.

A proper clearing and rebalancing of this chakra is certainly a must, but the root cause of this problem is the person's fear of leaving the Earth plane. They may not even realize that the Ascension energies are descending upon them but they will get a sense that something is changing. They may fear these changes and start blocking these energies. What a person at this stage needs to realize is that these energies will not transform them off the planet overnight. It is just a beginning process that can take years to complete. There is no set timeframe for Ascension. It can happen in one year or over a lifetime, or in several lifetimes. No one ascends until they are ready and have finished what they came to do on Earth. So sit back, relax, and let the Ascension energies flow.

Conducting a healing and balancing the 12th Chakra requires a high vibration within the healer, or yourself, if you are doing a self-healing. Some intense meditation before you begin is suggested. Listen to *ARDAS*, burn some incense or do whatever it takes to put you in the highest spiritual state you can be. Place one hand over the Heart Chakra and the other just above the Crown Chakra at the top of the head. Think the affirmation, *"From the highest river flows life."* It is an energy thought form that unlocks the 12th Chakra and will bring it into balance.

It would be good to do a 12th Chakra balance once every two months if you are having problems with this chakra, until it stays on track. Generally speaking, problems with the 12th Chakra fix themselves if left alone, however you may want to hasten the healing and alignment process with some healing work. If you want to help the 12th Chakra spin, place a diamond or a small clear quartz crystal with the point facing up, away from the feet, on the Brow Center (Third Eye) and then hold a clear quartz crystal over the Crown Chakra and you should be able to read the energetic information in the 12th Chakra.

You will be given the ability to discern the condition of a chakra from a six-sided clear quartz crystal. You can also use a small quartz crystal, six-sided, tied to the end of a string. You hold it over the Brow Chakra and see what it does. If it spins clockwise in a large circle the Twelfth Chakra is open and functioning normally. If it rotates in a small circle, the chakra is partially open. If it moves side to side the chakra is partially blocked. If it does not move at all the chakra is closed and not functioning. If it rotates counterclockwise it indicates the chakra is blocked with negative energy. The chakra can be dormant but working fine. The individual has not yet reached a point where this chakra is ready to open.

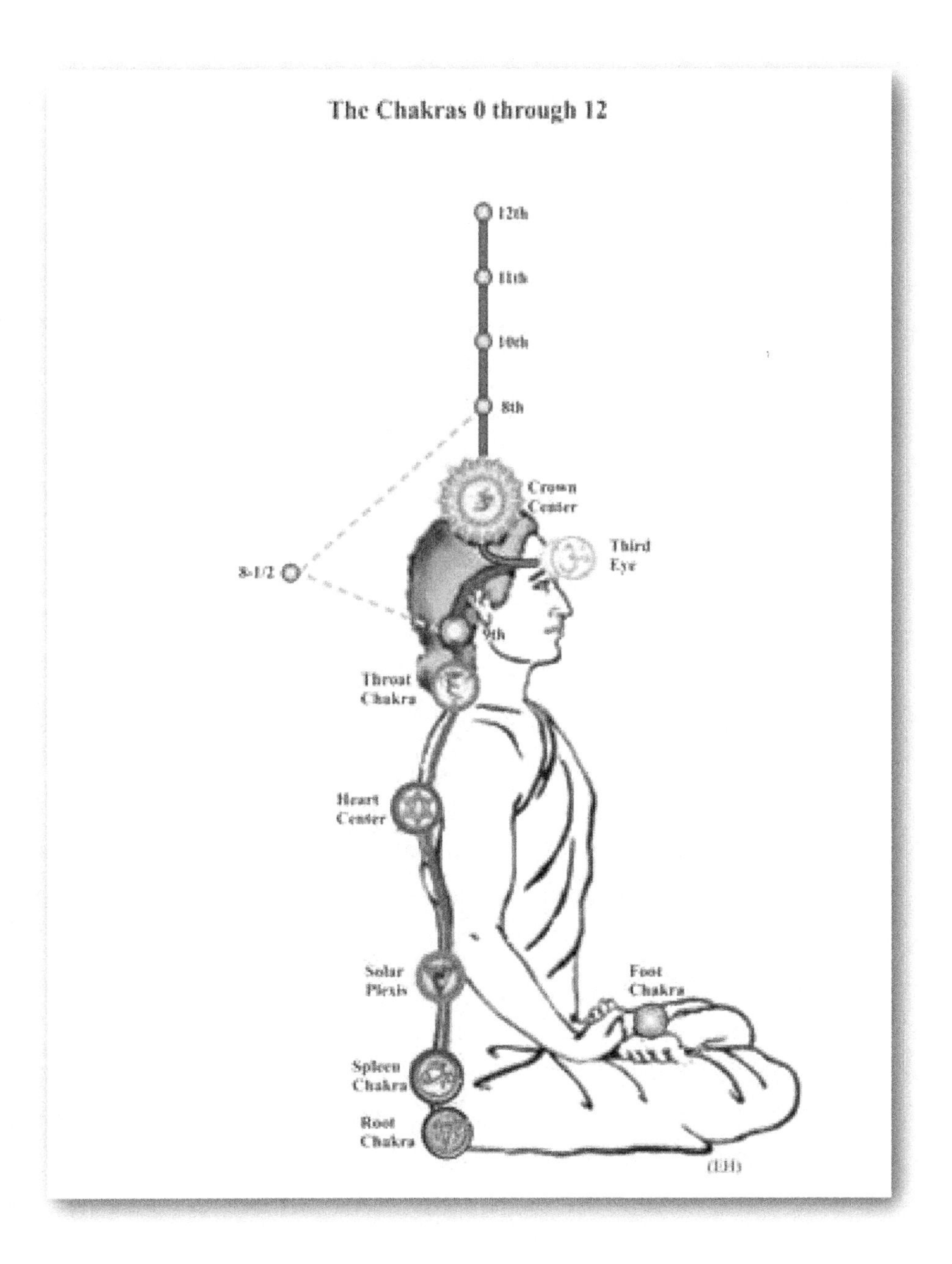
The Chakras 0 through 12
12th
11th
10th
8th
Crown
Center
Third
Eye
8-1/2
9th
Throat
Chakra
Heart
Center
Solar
Plexis
Foot
Chakra
Spleen
Chakra
Root
Chakra

Notes on The 12th Chakra

IX

Placement of the Spiritual Chakras

Thousands of years ago, our spiritual guides gave us some tools to help us grow spiritually. However, Spiritual knowledge is not static; it evolves as we do. New information arrives when we are ready to receive it. This is why so much new information is coming in at this time.

If you know what a *Chakra* is, then you probably know that there are seven of them and that they have a corresponding color, or vibration. This knowledge has been with us for thousands of years. And for thousands of years, it was true. But as we evolve and Ascend, the chakra system evolves as well. The ascended, fourth-dimensional or partially ascended human, has twelve chakras. They differ in many ways from the seven chakras of the Third Dimension, changing from seven tones to twelve, a lot like changing music modalities. The vibrations are different. The colors are different. The sound and the harmony are different and of course, the whole being is different. This higher vibration requires and creates the entire being to open, change, and become different.

If you are a healer, you will find that some people have activated all twelve of their chakras, while others still operate within the seven-chakra system. If any of the twelve chakras have been activated, then the individual is at least half the way to living in a Fifth Dimensional reality. Please note that when working with the twelve chakras, it is imperative that you begin clearing with the Crown Chakra and work upward.

What are the New Chakras and their color correspondences? Let's start from the top and work our way down.

Twelfth Chakra

Color: Diamond/Crystal Clear
The Twelfth Chakra is four levels above the Crown Chakra and engages us with Source, and your Blessed Higher Self, as it meets the human energy field, or Universal Body, just outside the Auric Field. This chakra is associated with masculine energy—"Father." It is our connection to our Soul and to the Spiritual Source of the higher levels beyond the Fifth Dimension.

Eleventh Chakra

Color: Turquoise/Silver
The Eleventh Chakra is three levels above the Crown Chakra. It corresponds with the mid-point of the Universal Body. It encompasses all of the lower chakras, so it must remain clear or all of the chakras will become out of balance and cause problems. While the Twelfth Chakra corresponds with the masculine, the Eleventh Chakra corresponds with feminine energy—the Christ-consciousness of Mother Mary, Kwan Yin, or Mother Earth. Its deep silver/turquoise energy radiates outward and encompasses parts of the Universe other than ourselves, so it is associated with balance, kindness, compassion, and connection with all life, including our Solar System and Mother Earth.

Tenth Chakra

Color: Bright Amber Yellow/Silver

The Tenth Chakra is one level above the Eighth Chakra, just outside of the auric field. Its energy radiates infinitely in a linear plane in all four directions: front, back, left, and right. Therefore, it is the chakra that connects us with everything. It also filters and protects the Higher Mind processes. This chakra is tied to the Golden Triad and the chakra where you link into the Golden Triad. (See: Pg. 136)

Ninth Chakra — at base of skull

Color: Magenta/Silver

The Ninth Chakra is the Pineal Chakra. It is the portal to the rest of the body, the Universal Body, as it will be the telepathic and levitation power point of the Fifth Dimension energies. It is also the upper Root Chakra, where creation and manifesting energy live. As such, issues about self-denial, feeling undeserving, fear of accomplishment and frozen growth will show up here. Its magenta/silver ray radiates as a cone, with the point of the cone beginning at the Third Eye, then spreading outward at the back of the head, located between the two occipital bones at the top of the spine.

Interfacing Chakra — 8 1/2

Behind the Head at soft spot
Color: Amber/White

There is a half-spin chakra between the Eighth and the Ninth Chakra, spinning at a lower rate. This chakra brings a clear triad connection between the Third Eye, Ninth Chakra and the Crown, and it governs emotional and mental clarity. Problems with any of these areas usually show up here, and express itself as a Fifth Dimensional headache. This Chakra vibrates half in the Fourth Dimension and half in the Fifth

Dimension. It is your bridge to accessing and ascending to the higher levels, and is carefully filtered by Amber and her legions of Angels.

Eighth Chakra

8' above the Crown Chakra
Color: Silver/Mother of Pearl
The Eighth Chakra, located 8' above the Crown Chakra, in the new fourth level of the aura, the color you will see is amber/gold within this new aura level, and this is the fuel that feeds the Third Eye, or inner vision. It is the foundation for the higher chakras and must be kept clean and clear. Its silver/ultra-violet, seen as clear ray radiates as a cone, with the point of the cone beginning at the Third Eye, then spreading upward through the Crown Chakra, finally connecting to the Blessed Higher Self and your Soul School guides.

Seventh Chakra

The Crown Chakra
Color: Gold/Violet
The Seventh Chakra is the Crown Chakra. It is about speaking your truth without judgment or delineation. Its color is Violet-Silver-Gold—Golden Truth. Use this color in healing when people need help understanding that their voice—every voice—creates a vibration and really matters. Whatever we think and say creates our karma while affecting our spiritual growth and future.

Higher Light Integration
This is the beginning of the rebuilding of your energetic fields and DNA. All the "clutter" has been cleared away and now the rebuilding can commence. This healing and alignment is done on the body table and can be very energizing. The axiatonal lines of force on the

Universal body are to be rewired and repaired if necessary. The axiatonal system is a vast network of grids linking you to your Higher Self, Oversoul, I AM Presence and Source. Axiatonal Alignment provides a direct link between Cosmic Intelligence and individual consciousness.

Three-dimensional filaments are placed within some of the chakras and the Universal energies are infused throughout the body and energy fields. The brain pathways are rewired to accept higher dimensional information and the Crown Chakra is connected to the Blessed Higher Self via the Eighth and Eleventh Chakra.

If it has not been done before—then the activation of the remaining crystals are accomplished in a healing/alignment session and a connection to the higher Light energies of the Spiritual realms are performed. This phase can take up to three hours depending on the client. Sometimes we have to "rest" and take time out for the process to continue safely, as clients can become disorientated and burned out; it is important that you remain "Present".

STEP ONE: The Karmic /Universal/Soul Re-absorption

This is the "big one" because this is when you release all the lessons your Soul has experienced that are no longer required. The Soul is on Earth to learn and experience specific things in life, but when you have learned all you need you can't seem to switch it off unless you are a very enlightened Soul. This is where the Universal Body surgeon facilitates the disconnection of the lessons in the double helix DNA spiral system. (You need to unhook these attachments from the spine) Do not think that you will have an easy ride after this. Releasing lessons opens a vortex and can allow others to come to the fore. The Vibrational Healing process clears out many things that have long since been redundant, but are still running and taking energies from more up-to-date processing. So many people are stuck.

Many of the lessons released initially are contained in the Karmic Nodes of the Moon, the polarities of our Universe—the parent/child syndrome. We all had parents and some of us have children. Teacher/student is another, and at some time we have experienced both facets of this. Unless you "finish" with them they are still running.

Vibrational Healing is the final part of the necessary Universal bodywork, as it signifies the end of the building. Your Soul will know when you are ready for a Vibrational Healing, but it must be done within three months of the healing release. The etheric Universal Body needs to be at a high vibration rate to release the Karmic/Universal/Soul.

We recommend doing a Karmic/Universal/Soul and re-alignment every year or so to keep the "motor" tuned up. A Vibrational Healing tune-up usually takes between one and a half to two hours to complete.

STEP TWO: The Divinity Infusion

After the Vibrational Healing is complete, we perform the Divinity Infusion. This is a series of affirmations to connect to your Spirit to the higher realms and to enhance your life. Usually this is done at the same time as the Vibrational Healing and takes about an hour or two to complete. After the tune-up is complete, it is advisable to take three days off from the world, just chilling and relaxing while the healing and infusion reforms your energy fields. Pamper and indulge yourself a little.

STEP THREE: Enhancing

After the first two steps, new paths begin to appear to you. This is when further enhancements/attunement can assist you in developing your Universal life path. Prerequisite to the enhancements is the Vibrational Healing work. The Universal Light Spectrum Alignment is a super-vibrational healing, opening up further depths of your consciousness, rewiring the template and activating your Soul power and then bringing the Eleventh Chakra frequencies to a higher level. The Divine Purpose Crystal is also activated to manifest the Soul's true purpose. The structures activated during this powerful process are enhanced and expanded.

The *Arc of the Covenant, between the 10th chakra and 4th chakra* is rewired and activated, the Divine Purpose crystal within the Heart Center in the chest, and the Upper Chakras, is activated and augmented with the Akashic records of your Soul, at the 9th chakra. The twelve chakras are realigned and adjusted to allow the embodiment of your divinity to resonate with the Divine Human rising within you. The Shield of Enoch is activated within the upper Spiritual Chakras, which allows the heart charkas (Four and Ten) to open more easily.

This step can be extremely powerful for some people. I personally experienced a huge opening of consciousness for weeks afterward. It is advisable to take a few days up to a week off from worldly matters if you can. Toning and infusions of God energy occur and this may leave you disorientated. You can even leave the physical body for a period of time. This phenomenon can happen at the opening and spinning of any Spiritual Chakra. After this session, many physical effects can be felt and it is advisable to have a few days rest before resuming your life. (Listen to Richard Shulman's music — www.richheartmusic.com)

The Templar Grid is an activation of dormant structures within your aura fields and it gives a greater connection and flow between the Earth and the Higher Planes. Based on Cabbalistic principles, a multidimensional "Tree of Life" is built within the Etheric Template Field, connecting to the "Earth core" Etheric Chakra below the feet, and to the "Capstone" or Tenth Chakra above the head. Both of these chakras are outside the aura field. This prepares the energy pathways within the Universal body and template. On the central column, the first connection is to the base chakra (Root) then the Creative Chakra (Second), passing through the Solar Plexus and Heart Chakra it ascends to the Divine Purpose Chakra (Throat). It then moves up through the Throat Chakra before connecting with the Crown Jewel (Brow Chakra) through the Crown Chakra to the Heart Capstone, Tenth Chakra.

The side pathways, or right and left meridian lines, connect to the upper and lower control panels of the Universal body and to several "physical" organs as well as the higher dimensional structures. (Astral Devices-Preparation). A greater connection can be felt with clients, friends and loved ones after this process. When two or more people have undertaken the Templar Grid together, they "feel" very connected. Even when they are apart the connection is still there. This is not a Three Dimensional "cording" controlling connection, rather a sense of belonging to one another. For healers it can enhance their abilities and intuitive senses.

THE EMBRACING SPIRITUAL FRONTIERS PROGRAM™

A prerequisite to this healing program is the Universal bodywork achieved in the Spiritual Intensives and Divine Sittings. At least ten sittings are preferred before you begin the Ascension Chakra healing work. A certification is required

The Angelic Alignments connect you to Arcangel Michael and his Legions or Orders. I can only briefly touch on this here. This is what the Japanese refer to as Kuden, or *oral transmission.* This program level is about a connection to the Angelic orders, which no human can control. The choice comes from a Soul Level, so no one can go into detail about what will occur during the sessions. When the sessions are over you will be part of *the Orders of Archangel Michael.* You will have received something from the Divine that only you will know.

At this point, these healing sessions are on a one-to-one basis and it is advisable to have had a Vibrational Healing within three months of starting this. program A prerequisite is required to have completed all the work up to the Vibrational Healing and entering the training program, and it is better but not essential, that you have undertaken the Divine Grid work as well as had The Reconnection with the energies of Soloman. (Solomon, the wisest of all men, built the Temple in Jerusalem and reigned over Israel's golden age.)

You, as a person, do not choose what is best for you, but your Blessed Higher Self chooses.

On the next page is the *NEW Spiritual Chakras Chart*, which is the same as on the back cover, This chart shows the sutras to chant as the chakra is opening, the color of each chakra, the Divine Seal (See Ascension—Accessing the Fifth Dimension Workbook) as well as the spiritual gifts each chakra brings when it is spinning and in balance and harmony.

You can obtain a Chart of Ascension in color via email. Go to my website www.new-visions.com - then to the Prayer Room to order.

The Sutra and Body Organ Chart

Chakra	Seal	Sutras	Body/Organ
12th Chakra (Glows Bright like the Sun)	Infinity	Advanced Spiritual Skills Teleportation Bi-Location Father	Universal Body Ascension
11th Chakra (Aqua Blue)	Libra	Telekinesis Universal Love Mother Spiritual Realization	Soul Healing Unity
10th Chakra Higher Heart Center (Amber/Gold)	Gemini	Healing Power Forgiveness Merging Joy	Total Oneness Heart w/Heart
9th Chakra (Magenta)	Scorpio	Soul Blueprint Karma Akashic Records Higher Abilities & Decisions	Unlocks Spiritual Skills Pineal Left-Brain
8-1/2th Chakra (Amber)	E-MC(2)	Strengthens Aura Raises Vibrations 5th Dimension Energies Balance and Acceptance	Opens the Spine for Higher Vibrations
8th Chakra (Ultra Violet)	Taurus	Compassion Selflessness Telepathy Spiritual Skills	Desire for Service Higher Ego
Crown Center Chakra (Violet)	Sagittarius	Immortality Infinity Grace Bliss	Right Eye Auric Shield Ears
Third Eye Chakra (Indigo)	Aquarius	Knowledge Freedom Wisdom Clear-Seeing	Pituitary Nose Left Eye
Throat Chakra (Lt. Blue)	Pisces	Discernment Affluence Abundance Communication	Thyroid Lungs Alimentary Canal
Heart Center Chakra (Yellow)	Leo	Love Peace Harmony Laughter	Thymus Circulatory System
Solar Plexis Chakra (Green)	Capricorn	Will Power Integrity Gut Reaction [illegible]	Adrenals Stomach Gall Bladder
Spleen Chakra (Orange)	Cancer	Prana Union Receiving Creativity	Spleen Sexual Organs Sacral Lower Back
Root Chakra (Red)	Aries	Strength Security Foundation	Kidneys Spinal Column
Foot Chakra (Hunter Green)	Virgo	Grounding Stability Balance Earth Connection	Feet Legs Knees

(EH)

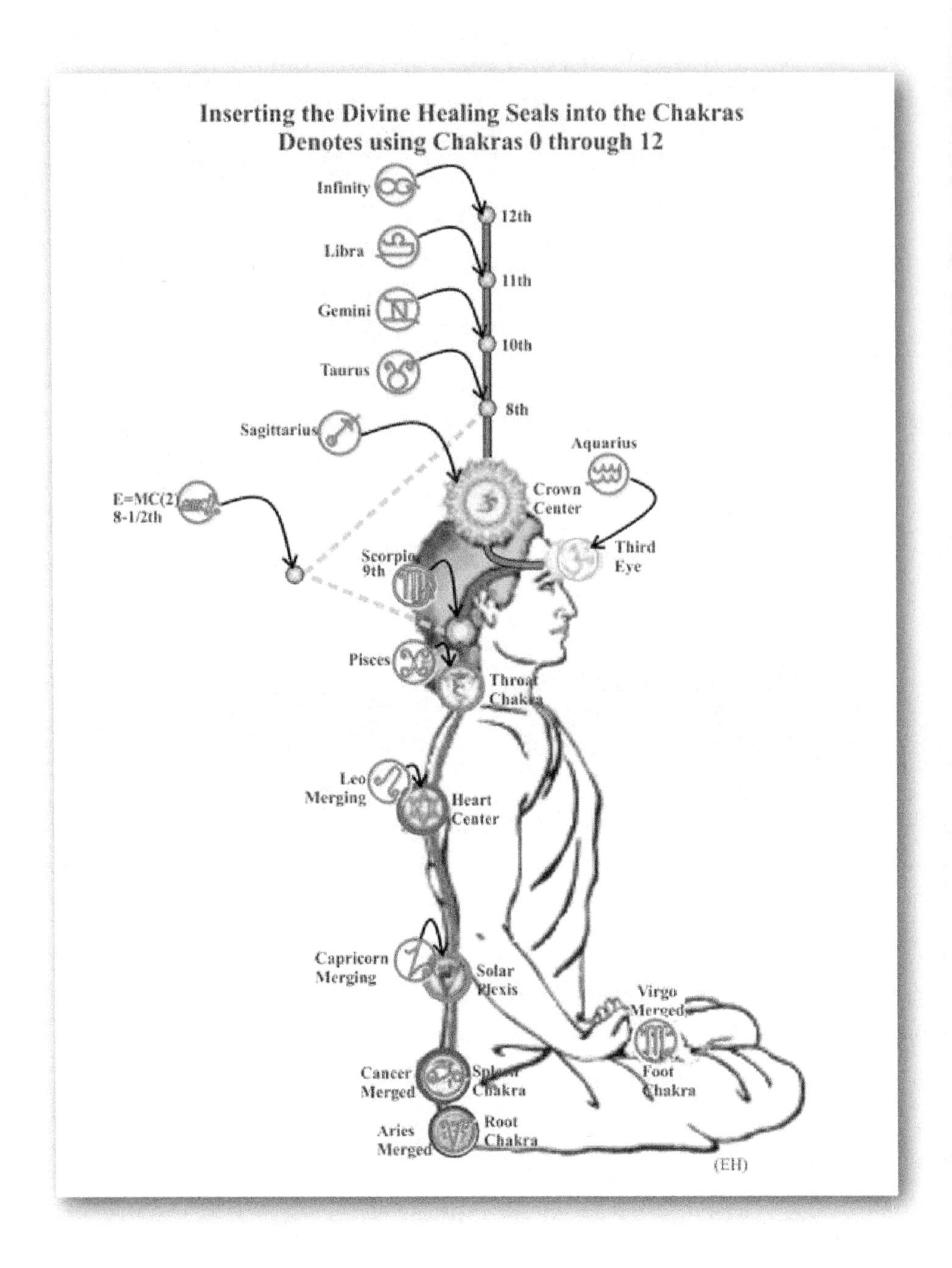
Inserting the Divine Healing Seals into the Chakras
Denotes using Chakras 0 through 12
Infinity
12th
Libra
11th
Gemini
10th
Taurus
8th
Sagittarius
Aquarius
Crown
Center
E=MC(2)
8-1/2th
Third
Eye
Scorpio
9th
Pisces
Leo
Merging
Heart
Center
Capricorn
Merging
Solar
Virgo
Cancer
Merged
Foot
Aries
Merged
Root
Chakra
(EH)

Invocation

To Unify the Entire Chakra Unit

I breathe in Universal Light
Through the center of my heart,
Opening my Heart Chakra
Into a beautiful ball of Yellow/Gold Light,
Allowing my Blessed Higher Self, my Universal Body,
To expand throughout my Aura.

I breathe in Universal Light
Through the center of my Heart Chakra,
Allowing the Light to expand,
Encompassing my Throat Chakra
And my Solar Plexus Chakra
In one unified field of Light
of Green, Yellow/Gold, and Blue
Within, through, and around my body.
To expand throughout my Aura.

I breathe in Universal Light
Through the center of my Heart Chakra,
Allowing the Light to expand,
Encompassing my Brow Chakra And my Navel Chakra
In one unified field of Light
of Green, Yellow/Gold, Indigo, and Silver
Within, through, and around my body.
To expand throughout my Aura.

I breathe in Universal Light
Through the center of my Heart Chakra,

Allowing the Light to expand,
Encompassing my Crown Chakra
And my Root Chakra In one unified field of Light
Of Red, Yellow/Gold, and Violet/Silver
Within, through, and around my body.
To expand throughout my Aura.

I breathe in Universal Light
Through the center of my Brow Chakra,
Allowing the Light to expand,
Encompassing my Eighth Chakra
Eight inches above my head
And my Ninth Chakra
Eight inches behind my head
In one unified field of Light
Of Indigo/Silver, Ultra-Violet, and Magenta/Silver
Within, through, and around my body.
I allow a Wave of Highest Consciousness
To move between these three points.
I AM One with Universal Light.

I breathe in Universal Light
Through the center of my Brow Chakra,
Allowing the Light to expand,
Encompassing my Eighth Chakra
(Eight feet above my head)
Around to my upper thighs
In one unified Circle of Light
Of Indigo/Silver, Ultra-Violet, and yellow/Gold
Within, through, and around my body.
I allow my emotional body to merge
With my physical body.
I AM One with Universal Light.

I breathe in Universal Light
Through the center of my heart,
Allowing the Light to expand,
Encompassing my Ninth Chakra
(Eight Feet Behind my head)
And my lower thighs
In one unified Circle of Light
Of Indigo/Sliver, Magenta/Silver, and Yellow/Gold
Within, through, and around my body.
I allow my consciousness and
The Universal Body to merge
With my physical body.
I AM One with Universal Light.

I breathe in Universal Light
Through the center of my Brow Chakra,
Allowing the Light to expand,
Encompassing my Tenth Chakra
(Twelve Feet above my head)
Around to my knees
In one unified Circle of Light
Of Indigo/Silver, Ultraviolet,
and Clear/Yellow
Within, through, and around my body.
I allow my spiritual Universal Body
and Chakras
To merge with my physical body,
Forming the unified field.
I AM One with Universal Light.

I breathe in Universal Light
Through the center of my Brow Chakra,
Allowing the Light to expand,

Encompassing my Eleventh Chakra
(Twenty-Four Feet above my head)
And my upper calves
In one unified Circle of Light
Of Indigo/Silver,
Deep Indigo Silver, and Yellow/Gold
Within, through, and around my body.
I allow the Universal Body to merge
With the unified field.
I AM One with Universal Light.

I breathe in Universal Light
Through the center of my Brow Chakra,
Allowing the Light to expand,
Encompassing my Twelfth Chakra
(Thirty-Six Feet above my head)
And my lower calves
In one unified Circle of Light
Of Indigo/Silver, Diamond/Clear, and Yellow/Gold
Within, through, and around my body.
I allow the Holy and Divine
Masters to merge
Within the unified field.

I AM One with Universal Light.
Through the center of my Brow Chakra,
Allowing the Light to expand,
Encompassing my Eleventh Chakra
(Twenty-Four Feet above my head)
And my upper calves
In one unified Circle of Light Of Indigo/Silver,
Deep Indigo Silver, and Yellow/Gold
Within, through, and around my body.

I allow the Universal Body to merge
With the unified field.
I AM One with Universal Light.

Within, through, and around my body.
Creating the fourth circle around my Aura Field.
I allow the Source's Presence
to vibrate and move
Throughout this unified field.
I AM One with Universal Light.

I breathe in Universal Light
Through the center of my Heart Chakra.
I ask that the highest level of my Spirit
To Radiate forth from my center,
The Fourth and 10th Chakras
Filling this unified field completely.
I radiate forth throughout this day.
I AM One with Universal Light.

I live within the Universal Light.
I love within the Universal Light.
I walk within the Universal Light.
I AM sustained and nourished By the Universal Light.

I joyously serve the Universal Light.
NOW I AM the Universal Light.
I AM the Universal Light.
I AM the Universal Light.
I AM—I AM—I AM.

I HAVE MERGED INTO THE ONENESS

MY SPIRITUAL CHAKRAS
HAVE OPENED
And I know that
We are all one.

I am harmonized within the
Universal Light.
Therefore, in the name of my
Spiritual Being,
I choose to become one with all;
I AM a wave of vibrating Light

My Light Body is One with
My Physical Body
Vibrating to the Frequency
Of the Fifth Dimension energies!

I AM

I humbly give thanks that this is complete.

δ

Notes on Integration of Chakras

Notes on Integration of Chakras

X

Embracing the Fifth Dimension Light and Energetic Changes

Everything in creation is *Light.* Your cellular structures and everything around you, the room you are currently sitting in or any other part of your reality, is all Light. Light exists at many different frequencies. There is visible Light and there is obscure or hyper-spatial, inter- dimensional Light. There are many different levels of Light. Light is all encompassing. *All of Creation is made of Light.* For this reason, every area of the body is highly Light sensitive. It is crucial that you understand and accept this point. We are all Light Beings. Even now, you could say that you are a Light Being having a human experience. We are now moving our awareness into a better position. From this new vantage point, we are able to see how the Spiritual Chakras operate.

To begin, let us examine the way your Crown Chakra connects to your now-forming Tenth through Twelfth Chakras. If you visualize the area around your head, you can see an energy triangle forming. Emanating from it are many vibrant, prismatic colors and energy information packets perceived as sudden blips of Light. This triangle connects the Twelfth (Universal masculine), Eleventh (Universal female) and Tenth Chakras. Another line travels from the Eleventh, to the Eighth

(Well of Dreams), to the Ninth (pituitary), and returns, back up to the Eleventh Chakra.

$$\nabla^2 A - 1/c^2 \; \partial^2 A/\partial t^2 = 0$$

The governing equation of matter waves traveling in space at velocity c.

Scalar Waves

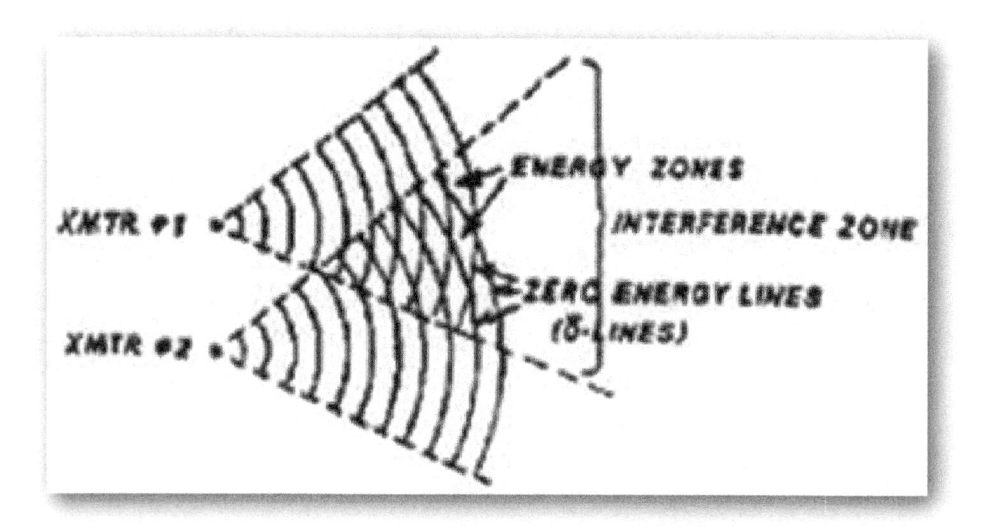

Visualize two flat circular shapes that connect through the Eleventh (Spiritual Crown) Chakra to create a special rotating-spin, *scalar wave* transducer. Scalar waves are inter- dimensional waveforms. The rotating, triangular head antenna allows an individual to radiate life and information-energy to others. Through this same device, the individual receives the energies of others. Both upper and lower brain centers are thereby able to telepathically inter-communicate in ways that are beyond the Third and Fourth Dimension's present capabilities. In effect, Earth humans will have first or *outer sight* and a complete second or *inner sight.* Psychic abilities such as telepathy, telekinesis, clairvoyance, clairaudience, and psychometry will become natural.

At this point, we will zoom our Third Eye camera focus out just a bit. From this macro perspective, we can clearly see how these centers interact. The Eleventh Chakra brings in Light (life and information- energy) and channels it to the Eighth (Well of Dreams) and Sixth (thymus) chakras. As we have just seen, the Eighth and Sixth centers (both Light sensitive) interact. *Remember that Life originates within the Divine Light of the Creator.* Focused in this way, many of the frequencies of Divine Light produce a Love harmonic vibration.

The energy this focus produces causes the Eighth and the Sixth centers to resonate with the Fourth (heart) Center. As the Eighth, Sixth, and Fourth Centers resonate with each other. They radiate energies that allow the Fifth (throat) Center to receive the incoming prana. (life energies). These harmonies (songs, vibrations of Light) move down to the prana or third (diaphragm) center, distributing the prana energy while invigorating and cleansing all the cells of the body.

These waves of energy cannot be regulated or controlled on this planet. They occur with Light and are unstoppable. The Spiritual Intensives and Divine Sittings, using Universal Light and the Divine helix, activate these waves of energy for healing. These scalar waves only stop when their purpose is accomplished.

From Arcturus-the new Interface Angel AMBER She is AMBER in color

The Angel Amber has come through the portal entrance at Arcturus, one of the most advanced civilizations in our galaxy. Edgar Cayce referred to Arcturus *as existing in the Fifth Dimension. It is the prototype for our Earth's future. Its energies work as emotional, mental, and spiritual – and as you contact this vibration from Earth you become healers for humanity.* This "star" is an energy gateway through which humans pass during death and re-birth. It is the gateway, *the Golden Door,* for non-physical consciousness to become accustomed to the physical body. *Arcturus is a Stargate* through which Souls pass, and where they chose to return to Earth or evolve elsewhere.

"Arcturus is the midpoint between Earth and the higher levels of consciousness. It is the governing body for our Universe, which determines the spiritual progress of humanity. Arcturus is the first docking station that allows us to travel beyond our limited Third Dimensional consciousness. Humans whose coded DNA has been activated by the Keys will be taken through Arcturus before moving on to other levels of creation.

According to the Arcturians, there are Twelve frequencies that correspond to our evolving Twelve—strand DNA. And then there's a Divine 13th that corresponds to the most powerful and purest vibration of Universal love and compassion. Our body's Seventh Chakra (crown chakra) connects us to the previous Six Chakras in our body and the new Foot Chakra (the Zero Chakra) into the Earth. Then an Eighth Chakra, about 12 inches above the crown, allows us to connect to a higher plane of consciousness."

—JJ Hurtak wrote in Keys of Enoch

A Ninth Chakra, located at the back of the neck and approximately two feet from the body, connects with the sacred grid work of the Earth. A Tenth Chakra aligns with the Solar System, an Eleventh with the Galactic Center, and a Twelfth with our physical Universe. A Thirteenth Chakra aligns with the super-galactic center that is a gateway for the most of the Ascended Masters and for the purest energies of the heart associated with the Divine Mother and Universal love. The Great Hindu Mother Ammachi is currently manifesting this energy in the physical and is a forbearer of the new energy to follow. Amma just explained the Eight and one- half Chakra to her students at the Ashram in India. Her

Yoga, the I AM Meditation, is the highest you can learn on the planet. (www.amma.org)

When you activate the Eighth Chakra, you gain the ability to explore a higher state of consciousness. When you activate the Ninth Chakra you can make contact with higher beings or guides who are still working in other frequencies on earthly planes, such as Mahavatar Babaci.

As the new codes of energy imprint themselves upon the crystalline structures of the Earth, changes within her will trigger systems in the body to follow suit because the human energy field seeks to maintain its umbilical connection with Earth Mother as well as the Universe. Such an effect is also seen in the way the structures of crystals realign when subjected to a new frequency, higher or lower.

When you activate the Tenth Chakra you can make contact with entities beyond the planet but in this Solar System—those who have shared some human characteristics but are also part alien. When you activate the Eleventh Chakra you can make contact with Sirians, Pleiadians, and the Arcturians. When activating the Twelfth Chakra, you can contact the Arcturians and also the higher-level beings such as those who are tasked with the Ascension of humans and the evolution of our galaxy. These Ascended Masters include Mahavatar Babaci and the White Brotherhood. The Thirteenth Chakra/Dimension, located above the Twelfth Chakra, activates the Super-Galactic Center, home of numerous galaxies and Universes where the *Galactic Federation* works from and where the female energies associated with Universal Love and fellowship manifest.

Notes on Energetic Changes

XI

The New Inter-Dimensional 12 Strand DNA

Scientific research has now proven that our DNA, known as a double helix configuration, holds the genetic codes for our physical and emotional evolution. Still to be discovered by science is the fact that our DNA has a much greater purpose than simply being a blueprint for our body, which is actually multi-dimensional.

The Human Genome Project (1989) decoded approximately 3% of the total physical DNA. The remaining 97% was then termed *"junk"*, inferring it has no purpose. We know that the human body is extremely efficient and anything that is of no use becomes atrophied and is evolved out of existence within a few generations. So, if 97% of our DNA is junk, why do we still have it?

That so-called *"junk DNA"* in your body contains all your history since you were first incarnated as a Soul, many lifetimes ago. It's where your *Akashic records,* the record of your Soul resides. Our DNA has been called a living library because of the wealth of information stored on it. The information holding these lifetimes in stored within your Ninth Chakra.

It's hard to believe, but lurking within your DNA are trillions of pieces of spiritual and biological energy in your body and much of these energies are *quantum.* They're inter- dimensional attributes of our inner selves, or cosmic Souls, and have hundreds of thousands of years of information stored within them. Learning how to access this information is key for the continuing growth and harmony of mankind.

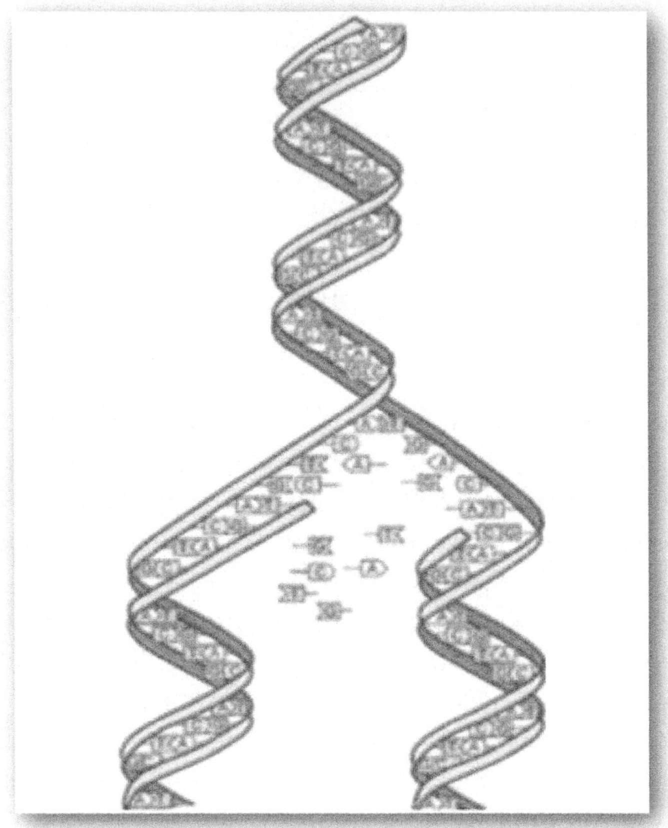

OUR DNA

There are ten additional strands of DNA that we have not opened ourselves up to as yet, *or five double helix strands*, which were disconnected or deactivated eons ago, perhaps after the fall of Atlantis. Science has yet to discover the purpose of these strands, although they have seen the shadows of them on their electronic microscopes. They call them "shadow DNA". Five strands for five dimensions.

With this Inter-dimensional 12 Strand DNA now coming available to us, you have to begin to access ten times the information available from your current DNA. These additional strands encompass the following areas of your life.

Connection to God/Spirit
Inner vision, receiving messages from spiritual guidance
Communication, both physical and spiritual
Love, both human and Divine
Physical Body
Life force energy (Shakti) and personal will

The Inter-dimensional 12 Strand DNA is ready to become activated and is unlike any other on the planet. The key to proper activation is working with your Spiritual Chakras and applying the *Divine Seals* to each chakra in a meditation exercise. This activates the 12 Inter- dimensional layers of energy that surround the DNA, connecting you to the 12 dimensions that are accessible to us now at this point in our evolution. (See: *Ascension—Accessing the Fifth Dimension Workbook.* Applying the Divine Seals is included in the Embracing Spiritual Frontiers™ program.)

You participate in the activation, experiencing the energy of it and making it more powerful. You'll be gently and carefully guided through the process by me and I'll be connected to you energetically to ensure that your activation is successful.

The Inter-dimensional 12 Strand DNA Activation utilizes color, the Divine Seals, and sound. The vibrations of the sacred seals open the receptors of your cells, allowing the activation to more easily be imprinted and activated within the DNA. Each Seal sets the vibration of the body at the correct rate to receive the activation at each level. The energy vibration of colors and Light adds to the power of this activation.

The Inter-dimensional DNA Activation is a powerful process that begins with a meditation exercise to center you and bring you into a relaxed yet focused meditation state. The DNA process is similar to a guided visualization or meditation. It includes the activation of all 12 strands of your DNA plus the activation of the 12 Inter-dimensional layers of energy that surround the DNA, activation of your Spiritual Chakras and the laying in of the Divine Seals.

The Inter-dimensional DNA Activation takes approximately one hour, including pre- instructions, the activation, and discussion afterward. The activation can be done by phone, Skype, or with Distance Healing.

Inter-Dimensional DNA

Your DNA has a much greater purpose than simply being a blueprint for your body. It contains all your history since your Soul first incarnated, many lifetimes ago. It's where your Akashic record, the record of your Soul, resides. As with everything in existence, the Akashic Record is in energetic or vibrational form. Your thoughts and actions, which are a form of energy, are recorded on your Akashic Record.

Thoughts that you repeat often enough compound and become beliefs. These beliefs are stored on the Akashic Record in the DNA in every cell of your body. According to the rate of the vibration of your beliefs, they can create good health or ill health. *This is the core, the root cause of all health conditions - good or ill.*

Every part of your body, bones, muscles, organs and glands have a specific vibration. In accordance with the *Law of Attraction,* thoughts are drawn to specific areas of the body that correspond with their *frequency.*

Application of the Divine Sittings prepare you to receive the Divine Seals and activate them within the 12 strands of your DNA. The first sessions will create some natural changes that are gradual and gentle. After several sessions people quit smoking, stopped drinking, get more friends, begin good eating habits, go organic, stop taking weight medication, start filtering water, and break addictions. They also gain employment and heal hurtful and painful relationships. All without trying!

The process of Inter-Dimensional Vibrational Healing is twofold:

First, remove the encoding of lower vibrational beliefs stored on your Akashic Record in your DNA. The programming of lower vibrating beliefs that are causing ill health and disease are removed from the physical DNA strands. Although clearing the beliefs from the physical strands is usually all that's needed, a check is performed using kinesiology to determine if they need to be removed from other specific area, such as one of the chakras as well.

Second, do not replace those beliefs. Allow the pure programming of the original, healthy DNA from the Double Helix DNA to take form in its higher, pure manner. The Master DNA Strand is also called the *Ascension Soul Blueprint* and contains original, perfect DNA encoding.

The *Inter-Dimensional Vibrational Healing*™ session is similar to the *Inter- dimensional 12 Strand DNA* session in that you'll actually be performing the healing process for yourself while I guide you through it by guided meditation. In particular the colors and Seals are used to enhance, embed, *and seal the vibrational healing into your DNA* and, thus, the Soul's Akashic Record.

In order to avoid a healing crisis, it's best to focus on only one or two health issues per session, and one Spiritual Chakra opening. Too much energetic change at one time in the body can overwhelm it, resulting in an upsurge of what appears to be ill health, but is actually a detoxification. This cannot be foreseen or controlled and a flair-up depends on the body's tolerance to the frequency adjustments. The discomfort of a healing crisis is caused by too much toxic waste—energetic or physical—being released from the cells as they become clear and healthy.

The 12 Strand DNA vibrational healing session takes approximately one hour, including pre-instructions, the process, and discussion afterward. The session can be done on the body table, by phone, SKYPE, or remotely with me.

Important! There is a three-day purification process before you can receive the Divine Seals for DNA Activation or prior to having a vibrational healing session.

Recoding to 12 Strand DNA or Double Helix

Medical science has established that we have 2 strands of DNA and 10 strands of "junk" DNA, but they have not understood the purpose of that "junk" DNA. Recent information has revealed its higher purpose; supporting a multidimensional consciousness, our Soul's natural state. Realigning, reconnecting and activating our 10 strands of junk DNA, or *the DNA Recoding Process,* is the process by which we attain that state. When we are multidimensional, our physic abilities are reawakened and we begin to develop a second neural universal network at the etheric level. This second neural network is what allows us to live in multiple dimensions at once. We can hear, see and communicate with our Galactic Neighbors in these higher frequency dimensions.

There are twelve levels in the *Divine Seals DNA Recoding Process* and each requires emotional clearing at the level that activates the thymus to change the coding sequence of our DNA. Recoding in this instance means switching on the forty-four DNA codes that were previously switched off. You could liken it to remodeling your body at the cellular level while still living in it.

The DNA Recoding process works at the etheric—some call it the Universal Body—level. At this level your 10 strands of junk DNA along with your 2 connected strands are realigned at the 8th Chakra, above your Crown Chakra. Because DNA is holographic, it can be simultaneously realigned, reconnected and activated. This means that your 10 junk DNA strands are simultaneously realigned above the top of your head (crown), reconnected into your 12th Chakra energies and reactivated so that life force energy, or Shakti, flows through them again.

Once your 12 DNA strands are plugged back into your Physical Chakras by way of your Spiritual Chakras, your Angelic Recoding Guide's jobs are nearly complete. They will continue to watch over you and monitor your 12 strand reconnection until you reach the frequency needed to fully activate the reconnection. The Activation of the 12 strands happens in 3 steps:

1. Activation of the Crown Chakra and Eighth Chakra. You will feel this as an itching or tingling at your Crown Chakra.
2. Activation of the Tenth Chakra energies or antenna. The Tenth Chakra antenna is used to receive messages from other dimensions.
3. Activation of the Hypothalamus. This is the *Universal Translator* and translates all messages into your chosen language. Messages are received as *frequency thought-forms.*

Many are complete with emotions, pictures and language. Some have only one or two of these. The Hypothalamus also provides you with the identity of the sender. After receiving for a while you will learn to identify the senders and what galaxy or area of the Universe they are from. Once the hypothalamus is activated the activation process is complete and your DNA chart is also completed. Proof is visual (aura photos), emotional (not holding negative emotions in the body-becoming neutral), and physical (feeling more in control of your power and hearing messages daily).

Since so many people will be requesting The Divine Seals DNA Recoding, I have created a self-actuated meditative process. As you meditate, you'll receive off-world assistance from an Angelic Genetics Engineer. These are normally beings from Acturia. You will also be given a Divine Seal DNA Recoding Guide to see you through the process. Earth-based free assistance is also provided. This support group is where recoders go to get help from others in moving through the Ascension Recoding process.

Our entire solar system and the Milky Way Galaxy, has now entered a highly charged portion of space. We are immersed within the Photon Belt (Menasic Radiation), a period of intense light we first entered in the late 1990s and where we will remain for a 2,000 year period. During this remarkable time the energies from the Photon Belt are triggering a complete reordering of life as we know it. This occurs because *photon light energy has the capacity to lift all of life into a higher frequency dimension* as it carries the upgrade codes for the enlightenment of all. The atomic structures within the cells of our bodies are slowly re-tuning themselves to match these rising frequencies. We are shifting from a third dimensional carbon-based body, one that matches the atomic frequency and spin of carbon, to a fifth or higher dimensional crystalline body or *Universal Light Body,* one that matches the atomic frequency and spin of crystal. So too the bodies of animals, plant life and all upon and within the earth are making this transition, as is our entire galaxy.

Double Helix DNA

As the process of rebuilding our Universal Light Bodies continues we will slowly begin to notice the effects of becoming fully conscious or multi-dimensional. This state will come about when our 12 strands of DNA have finally been re-fused, reconnected and aligned and activated with our Spiritual Chakras. We will then experience life within the consciousness of multi-dimensionality. In this level of consciousness we could live in the third dimension while retaining our connection and relationships with beings in dimensions within the higher realms. We will no longer be cut off from other dimensions as we presently are, and we will operate from a state of heart-centered compassion, (Christ consciousness). This will happen regardless of which dimension we find ourselves inhabiting.

Eventually we will learn how to live successfully in a *galactic society* and ultimately in a Universal society. At the present time most humans have two active strands of DNA, represented by an intertwined double helix. Some of us have developed and integrated three or more strands and a large number of new babies presently being born (the indigo and crystal children) have many strands of active DNA. A simple blood test can verify this fact.

Each of the 12 DNA strands represents one of the twelve aspects of multi-dimensional consciousness and the Twelve Chakras. Three DNA strands represent and govern the physical body, another three are concerned with the emotional body, another three with the mental body, and the remaining three with the spiritual body. All these aspects are represented in our bodies as new neural pathways to the brain. They are connected and nourished through the endocrine system of ductless glands. Each gland is connected to a chakra. These glands work in tandem with the energy vortexes within our bodies and etheric energies, known as the Chakra System. When all neural pathways are working freely with our Chakra System, they will provide the conduit to the higher realms, resulting in our experience of inter-dimensional consciousness.

Developing the NEW Chakra System

We live in a Universe propelled by the laws of electricity and magnetism and all third dimensional life forms within it reflect this. Our stars and planets (geo-magnetic life forms) all have a north pole and a south pole with magnetic lines of force flowing between them. Our human bodies (bio-magnetic life forms) also conform to this bi-polar magnetic field, with the top of our head reflecting our north pole and the soles of our feet, our south pole. In a third dimensional representation, these lines of force moving between our head and feet completely encompass the body within an etheric structure known as a tube torus or *aura*. Imagine this donut shaped energetic field extending fully around your body. It is commonly known as your *aura*.

Have you noticed that when meeting another person for the first time you may be instinctively drawn to them? This is evidence that both of your auras are vibrating in sympathetic vibrational resonance. The same would be true when the presence of another feels uncomfortable. Perhaps the electro-magnetic energies in your auras are repelling each other. This can be dangerous if the vibration levels/spins are far apart. At the center of each bi-polar magnetic field is a magnetic core running from north to south. In the case of a simple bar magnet it is a magnetized piece of metal. In the case of the bio-magnetic human body it is a channel, only observable in subtle matter, called the midline or pranic tube. Within this core the life force is carried to sustain each individual creation during its existence.

Every spiritual tradition identifies and acknowledges the life force, that great field of potential energy that gives rise to and then sustains everyone and everything in existence from moment to moment. This energetic force is everywhere, vibrating at various frequencies, continually, every second in time and out of time. In Chinese spiritual teachings, the life force is called chi, while the Japanese and Koreans call it ki, (Rei*ki*, healing with the life force). In the Tibetan traditions it is identified as prana and the Hindu's call it Shakti. The Christian tradition names the life force, sanctifying grace or *Grace.* Practitioners of new age spirituality refer to this field as the Light or the White Light, and to the physicist, it's known as the sub-atomic or *quantum field.*

At this time the life force is also being intensified and expanded by the Photon Belt. As you move among numbers of people going about their business in any large city, you can notice and identify many of those who are suffering from a diminished access to the life force. It shows in their state of health, their sense of openness and self-confidence and even the way they relate to others and carry themselves. We must all access the life force fully and completely to maximize its benefits to our daily existence. Our complete Chakra System is the vehicle that has been beautifully designed to fulfill this function.

The Chakras and the DNA Connection

Chakra is a Sanskrit word that translates as "a spinning wheel of light." It is one of many human names for what is perceived to be a biophysical connection to our soul or spirit. These energy connections or chakras exist in that the soul or spirit is immersed in the physical body and mingles throughout. At present we each have seven of these energy connections that are woven into our body's meridian centers with some lying along the spine. These centers are similar in function to the junction box found in the electrical system of a home or office. Our physical body is also controlled through a vastly complicated neuro-electrical circuitry, with a number of special locations where these circuits converge. Each of these locations is monitored through a special mini neuro-computer connected through the central nervous system to the brain. It is these specific locations that are called chakras and each fulfills several functions. As well there are certain endocrine glands associated with the functioning of each chakra. And since the vibratory field of light also activates color and tone, each of the chakra centers produces its own specific color and sound. (See *Ascension- Accessing The Fifth Dimension.*

The DNA Strands and Endocrine Glands

Each of the following twelve DNA strands represents one of the twelve aspects of multi- dimensional consciousness.

Strand 1: Courage to move ahead and integrate our fears
Strand 2: Ability to focus on something and follow it to completion
Strand 3: Maintaining gender balance between male /female power
Strand 4: Balance between our energy field and the physical body
Strand 5: Living peacefully in a state of acceptance
Strand 6: Strength to stand in one's truth regardless of the outcome
Strand 7: Ability to accept both our dark and light sides
Strand 8: Ability to hold personal boundaries regardless of outcome
Strand 9: Ability to accept and live within a diverse community

Strand10: Ability to tune into and listen to one's Soul or Blessed Higher Self
Strand 11: Power to envision, create and manifest these visions in 3D
Strand 12: Ability to be accepting, kind and appreciate the value in all things

The Pineal Gland, DNA activation and The Endocrine Glands

Hypothalamus — I translate what I believe
Pineal — I see or envision what I receive
Pituitary — I hear what I receive
Thyroid — I speak what I receive
Thymus — I clear and transmute what I receive
Heart — I feel what I receive
Gonads — I create and manifest what I receive
Adrenals — I hold true to what I receive

In the recoding process each strand must be individually reconnected to each gland and then activated. This provides the DNA upgrade needed to sustain full consciousness and communication with the higher realms. These aspects are represented in physicality as new neural pathways to the brain and when the connection is completed our multi-dimensional consciousness will be fully felt and accessed.

The light from the Photon Belt entering through our pituitary and pineal glands is primarily driving this recoding process. This light stems from the Ninth Chakra at the back of the head, between the two occipital bones. It is important to note that *we are being reconnected very slowly* otherwise our physical bodies and our nervous systems could 'burn out' and we would not survive. We can actively co-operate in this process by trying to reach some understanding about what is happening to us. *Our ability to interact with and absorb the new frequencies of light into our physical bodies will determine how we progress in this next step of our physical and spiritual evolution.* And by carefully observing our belief systems and our actions, while using caring, neutrality, and will as the fuel to advance spiritually, we will change and clear many undesirable old thought forms and patterns that no longer serve us. We also must work with our Chakra Systems daily to strengthen our new aura and entire magnetic field.

Be wary of those who offer techniques to hasten or unduly advance your DNA recoding, particularly if these carry a large price tag. Many higher beings, angelic guides, and masters are actively involved with us at this time. They are assisting each of us in this recoding process so try not to rush ahead. This procedure cannot be hastened by anything that we can read in a book or buy in a bottle. It is occurring in exactly the right time frame regardless of how we might try to interfere or speed things up.

This scenario is immense and includes our entire Milky Way Galaxy. It is happening in response to the Divine Plan for our Universe, initiated by the Creator. So relax and go with the flow, allowing all of it to manifest in its own good time. Enjoy the ride. The final results will be awesome and will usher all of us into an inter-dimensional experience of living with compassion in Heaven on Earth.

A newborn baby immediately begins to have a relationship with the parents, doctor, siblings, and the extended family members. When the child goes to school, they develop relationships with classmates, teachers, and others. As an adult they develop relationships with many, many people. As long as you are living in this lifetime, on this earth plane, you will have relationships.

Relationships are a very important part of humanity because through them, the Soul is able to either expand and grow, or shrivel on the vine. Each one of us is deeply affected by relationships with our loved ones and friends as well as with various organizations, relationships between your neighborhood, state, and the country where you live as well as relationships between countries.

There are many teachings, books, workshops, and seminars about relationships. Hopefully, this writing will explain the secret of transforming your relationships at the Soul level.

The one Truth to transformation of relationships is: *Go within and transform the Soul of the relationship first, then the outer, physical part of the relationship will automatically follow.*

It is very difficult to find a person who has not struggled at one time or another with a problematic relationship. Some may struggle their entire life with relationships. What is the root cause of blockages within our relationships? The answer is always one answer, **Karma.**

When you learn about the new energy on the planet, the energy streaming from the center of our galaxy and the double helix, you will begin to understand the power of the Circle of Light. During meditation, if your Spiritual Chakras are open enough, you will be able to access the Circle of Light, and enter into it to begin to heal yourself and change history. This energy gives you access to the *Divine Book of Life* as well as the *Akashic Records.* This ability offers Spiritual guidance to many people with relationship challenges. If blockages to relationships are related to karma, then clearing your karma can and will make a big difference in your relationships.

When you have blockages with your spouse, your children, your relatives, your boss, your best friend, know and understand that there is always a Spiritual reason for these blockages, either from this current lifetime or because of a past life experience.

Accessing the Powerful Fifth Dimension Circle of Light

We have all shared relationships in our past lives, that come back into our life in this present lifetime, not only as a husband and wife perhaps, but as friends, mother-son, father-daughter, employer and employee, brother and sister. The current relationship and its blockages will be related to one or two of these past lifetimes. The Souls recognize each other at the cellular level, which is called *molecular recognition.* If they are from the same Soul Pod School, then they are in each others life as a gift, and for one reason only, for the growth of both Souls. This reunion was determined to occur in the present lifetime, at the exact time that it does, before both Souls entered their present lifetime bodies.

The proper use of the Circle of Light is the most powerful meditation on the planet at this time. It can heal troubled relationships, heal the sick, and erase karma if you go deep enough. It is able to access *the Double Helix Light* at the center of our galaxy. You can begin to use the Circle of Light once your Eighth Chakra has opened.

I use these techniques and access this energy at my quarterly intensives, and the results have proven to be more than amazing.

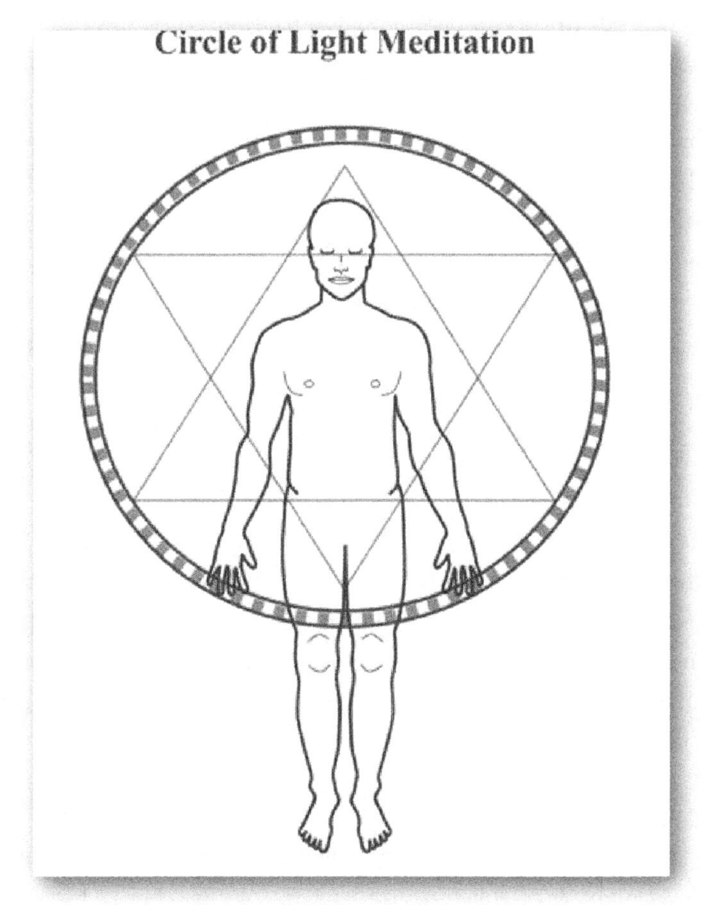

The Love and guidance for both of these Souls is to purify their hearts with love, care, compassion, and offer unconditional forgiveness to each other as well as to themselves. The significance of forgiveness between two Souls reunited in this way cannot be overstated. There cannot be any deep and long-lasting healing until each one has been able to purify and unconditionally forgive the other. This action releases any current blockages between them and heals on a very deep, focused level.

When you access the Circle of Light and raise your frequency up to that level of Light, it brings in an immediate Divine Presence and creates the ability for *Soul conferences.* This experience is similar to Skyping on your computer. This exercise should be done with the guidance of a teacher until you have learned to master the energies involved.

By consistently going to the Soul of the troubled and blocked relationship and healing on that level, will have a great impact in your outer world, both with the other person and with many other relationships in your life as well. The results can be dramatic and love and compassion will begin to flow between you, naturally. You will also feel an abundance of gratitude coming in from many other relationships in your present life. The Soul guidance for both of these Souls is to undertake this deep healing to clear and release many past life long-standing issues.

As you go through this clearing experience, you are also setting the energy for your next lifetime yet to come. Remember, everything you experience in your present lifetime is recorded in the *Divine Book of Life,* and after you pass on, becomes a permanent part of your historic Akashic Record.

Atoms are created from the rays of Living Light and are gathered into form by thought. God gave a mind to each man with which to think, to dream, to form patterns of his own imagination by the living force energy of his own mind. All those thoughts will take form, to flourish or to die, according to the attention with which one's garden is nourished and sustained. This is why the Vision Board works and why the Circle of Light's healing is so powerful.

The Tree of Life is that which man holds within his own being at birth, *becoming a branch of the God force Tree of Life.* He is his own Eden, his Soul. Each man by the choices he makes and the selection of his own thoughts can bring forth abundance of all that his thoughts can embrace.

This Tree, of which man is a branch, produces and brings forth, for good or for ill, the result of his own thinking. Many produce a mixture of both love and hate of their own creating. *Therefore a man is what he thinks, not what he thinks he is!*

That man is judged by his thoughts is most assuredly true. He will be destroyed by his wicked, polluted, or selfish thoughts. A man is noble, mediocre, or completely defiled by the caliber of his thoughts. Man is and will be until the end of time, held accountable for the products of his mind.

This amazing mystery, or *mist-tree* has been ignored as man has tried to bolt and lock away from his mind the memory of how it produces. He has sought to close his eyes to his own responsibility with regard to the fruit of his tree and what is brought forth into his life as a result. He is only childishly thinking to be held unaccountable for his thoughts and actions.

This Tree of Knowledge is also the Tree of Death, for by its fruits came death into the world. He who only thinks selfish, angry, filthy, and defiled thoughts is required to live the life of his own corruption; degenerate, contaminated poisons of lust, dishonesties, or selfishness, will find that he is feeding upon his hates and evils. He will eventually consume himself and die, for this is the Tree that brought death to the world.

Every living Soul is fed and nourished upon the fruit of his own thinking, which is why it can be most difficult to pull yourself out of a wicked, abandoned, and loveless childhood. To grow, release, and create new thought forms that bring success, joy, fulfillment, and Love, would need to be created, lived, and experienced. This can be done, of course, and has been, but many times because of past life "good karma."

The fruits of the Tree can be glorious because man can change his thinking patterns! The Law itself is just, and the ability to choose to change one's habits is *mercy.* That which you visualize will be given to you. The fruit you produce through your thinking habits becomes your diet and the harvest of your own planting will come forth in time. You must first empty out, release, and erase all the negative thoughts from your being through meditation and energetic healing work.

When the two eyes become single and focus on Spirit—they become one—the Third Eye, and will be filled with Light. The harvest will become your own planting and what you will bring forth. Then there shall be no darkness in you.

As the Spiritual Chakras open, and Light begins to fill the forth level of your aura and filter into the physical body and reality, you will begin to comprehend all things, the first one being and knowing the *Law* which brings about all conditions, either good or evil, according to the inner vision and thoughts he holds within his mind. He will understand fully and with reverent awe, that he is a branch of this great Tree, and *therefore responsible for the fruit that he produces.*

What does an Inter-Dimensional Vibrational Healing session entail?

Universal Body Activation is done first to raise the *vibrational frequency* of the body so the DNA Activation can occur. Utilizing the Spiritual Chakras and energy work, the body's frequency is attuned to the optimal vibrational level of each individual for spiritual growth and self-transformation. This establishes resonating with our highest potential and greater empowerment of our Soul's process and unity. The 10 "shadow" DNA are activated through the opening of the 8th and 9th Chakras, which flow right to basic cells in the body.

Effects: The initial activation meditation *(The Spiritual Chakra Invocation)* moves you into the "Morphogenetic Field" where emotions, behavior patterns, and beliefs that are not serving you are replaced with the vibrational frequency of Unconditional Love, accelerating the necessary changes to consciously vibrate and live within your life's Blueprint. The Divine Seals hold the new vibration in place so it can take hold and grow stronger over a period of time. This is why the Divine Sittings are cumulative. *(See Ascension—Accessing the Fifth Dimension — Workbook)*

What are the benefits of Universal Body Activation?

- Strengthening of the immune system
- Detoxification of the body
- Have more energy, look and feel younger

- Release unconscious patterning
- Releasing emotions, behavior patterns, and beliefs that are dysfunctional while strengthening functional ones.
- Expanded awareness and increasing brain capacity
- Precise communication and sharper memory
- Stay focused and in the moment
- Heightened intuition, clairvoyance, and clairaudience
- Opening the Chakras and creating a greater flow of kundilini energy
- More clarity and alignment with your true Soul purpose
- Clearing genetic and family karmic patterns
- Forming new behavior patterns more in fit with the Universal flow

Accelerate Your Spiritual Journey with a Future Life Progression

You have heard about past life regressions in which you take a guided journey back into one of your past lifetimes to heal karmic issues. With the new energies, you can be treated to a *Future Life Progression,* in which we journey forward with the help of our angels and *Inter-Dimensional Soul Council* to a future lifetime in which we successfully master all our lessons and are living our true life's purpose.

Then we bring the energy of that future lifetime back into this lifetime to help us accelerate our spiritual growth.

You can make arrangements for a Future Life Progression by calling or e-mailing the Center at 201-934-8986.

E-mail: Elizabeth_joyce@verizon.net

THE GOLDEN TRIAD—Standing in the vibration of the Fifth Dimension

Post this chart up in your healing room to help you become familiar with the Divine Seals, the charkas they correspond with, as well as the body organ and Sutras.

The Golden Triad

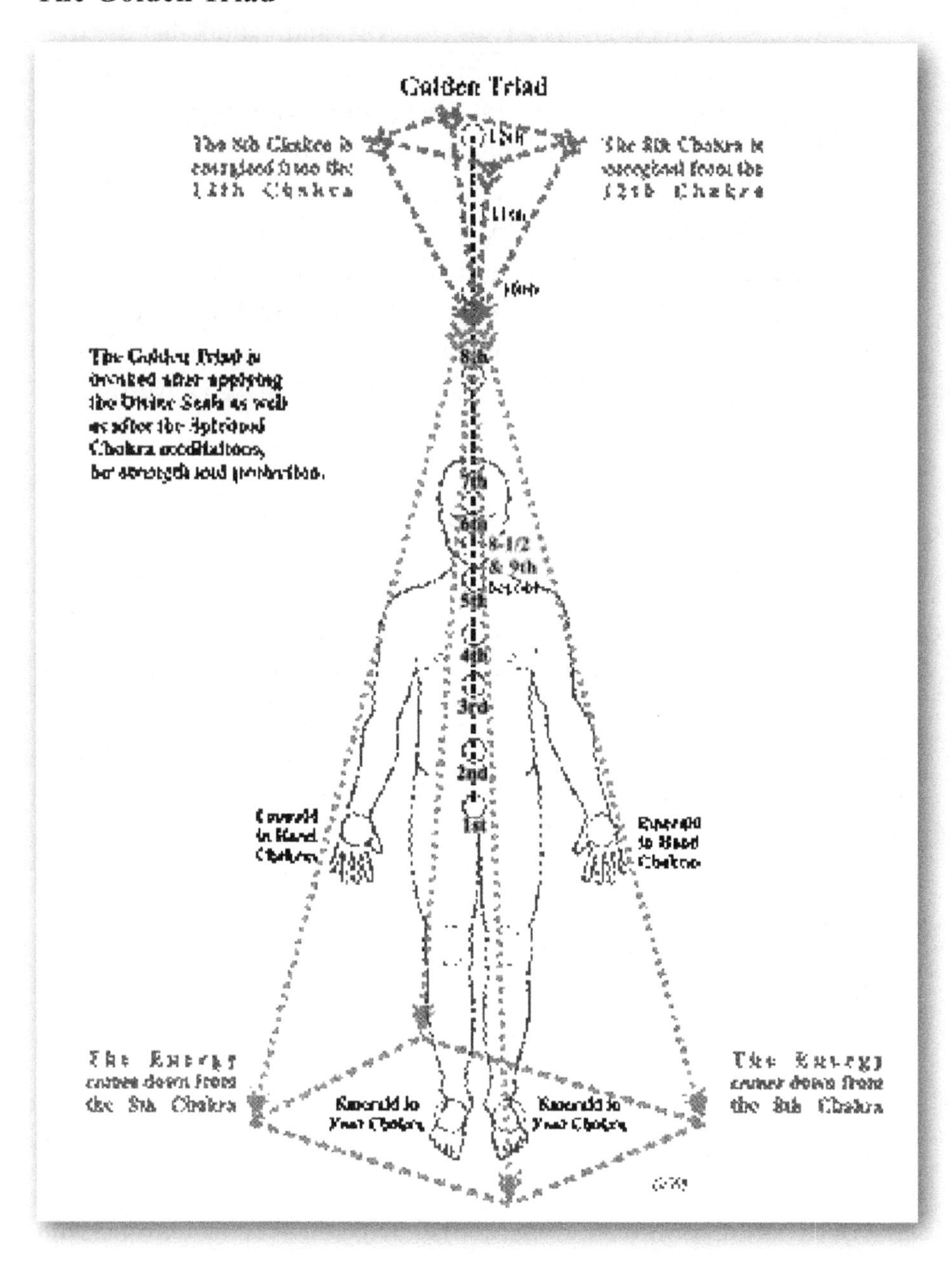

Notes on The New Inter-Dimensional 12 Strand DNA

Notes on The New Inter-Dimensional 12 Strand DNA

XII

Oneness Exercises

Exercise One
Emotional Alignment
Purpose: Mood matching

To better understand your spouse, friends, or co-workers in an effort to create peaceful conditions in your lives.

Pair up and sit face to face with your partner.

Take turns *scanning* each other's energy telepathically, looking for emotional vibrations. The person being scanned sits quietly with eyes closed, and projects energy toward scanner. The scanner has eyes open and may use telepathy, and aura reading abilities to come up with conclusions. Share your results, and thank your partner for his/her insights

Exercise Two – Mental Telepathy
Purpose: Experience the Oneness vibration

To detect the power of your connection to each other.

Pair up and sit face to face with your partner.

Take turns sending a number between 1 and 5 to the other's Third Eye.

The sender and the receiver both have their eyes fixed on each other's Brow Chakra or Third Eye.

Share your results, and see how close you are to achieving Oneness by detecting the correct number, or coming close to it.

Now surround your team in protective white light. Perceive the unit of One that you have created, and try the exercise again.

How do your results differ from before the addition of White Light and higher energies?

Exercise Three
8th Chakra Meditation

Purpose: To open and spin the Eighth Chakra

Sit in a chair with both feet flat on the ground, legs uncrossed. Make sure your spine is straight. Close your eyes and visualize yourself standing amidst the most Rainbow-like beautiful energy. Visualize yourself standing in the most beautiful amber-golden mist.

Take a deep breath.

It is important to feel very comfortable within this golden energy that takes on the shape of your energy field, beginning to rise up and connect you to your Spiritual Chakras. Take another deep breath.

See within your mind your Blessed Higher Self – your *Universal Body Self,* contained within the four levels of your Aura, and with that vision—claim yourself to be a powerful being by repeating the *Ascension Invocation for the 8th and 9th Chakras within your mind.* Claim yourself as a powerful healer, creator, and co-creator of this world, working alongside the ***One that Creates All;*** joining together and co-creating your life, your miracles, and your preferred existence here on Earth.

Take a deep breath.

Activate this beautiful amber/golden energy that you are enveloped in as you draw within the power and the strength to practice your intention by accepting the higher energetic vibrations and moving yourself into a whole new power of thought by allowing the Divine Will of the Supreme God Light to be integrated into your entire Universal Being.

Take a deep breath.

Now imagine a most beautiful silver energy manifest on the inside of the amber/golden energy, insulating the three original levels of your Aura, providing your amber/golden shield with a liquid silver energy.

Take a deep breath.

Remind yourself that you are an expression of fluid love as you become the flow of unconditional love towards the Self and all others. Remind yourself of the feminine aspect of the Universal Body that always supports you in the highest and best way for you to remain flexible, and in so doing, embrace *the Fifth Dimension harmonies,* the flexible side of your personality, by allowing the Creative God Light to create within you the energetic vibration that is needed for you to transform your life.

Take a deep breath.

Now connect your heart center energy to the silver and amber/golden energies. If you need to place your hand on your heart to connect to the reality of your pulsating heart do so, once again connect to the pulse of your heart.

Connect your heart energy to the heart of your etheric plasma, the Universal Body, thus connecting your beating heart to the amber/gold and silver lining around your aura, attached to the 9th Chakra at the back of your head. You do this by sending unconditional love into this area —the part of your physical reality forming your etheric outline— therefore with every beat of your heart send unconditional love into the spaces that exist between the spaces that surround you.

Fill your auric field with this amber/gold and silver light. Send this light-love vibration to fill up all of the particles of light that exists between your non-and-physical localities.

Take a deep breath.

Visualize your entire energy field filling up with Light and love as you to visualize your entire energy field also filling with soft pink and amber/gold on the outside of your energy field. (From Amma) and the silver on the inside edge (the fourth level of your aura) of your energy field. Allow the pink Amma energy to fill up your energy field as it carries this light frequency and sound of unconditional love. Allow it to infiltrate your etheric—Universal anatomy, as you float within the most exquisite and most beautiful plasma of etheric unconditional love.

Now—begin to visualize that the amber/golden energy that encapsulates the outside of your energy field sending triggers of energy toward your inner heart pulse; (4th Chakra) an energy that creates a sonic vibration of sacred sound and light as it births two golden spheres of energy that float from the 9th Chakra and come to lodge itself within your Heart and Root Chakra. The amber/golden vibration of your Universal Light Body gives of itself—creating a new golden energy star template lodged within your Heart and Root Chakras.

Take a deep breath.

You are now connecting with every Angelic and Archangelic energy known and unknown to you at the level of your Heart and Root Chakras.

Please understand that the time has come for you to *let go of the control you have over others by allowing them to let go of the control they have over you.* Begin to live through your heart, and make a point of shining your light towards others no matter their response. Connect to the *love crystals at the Heart Center*, allowing these energies to transform all of the energy that prevents you from claiming your magnificence as an Angelic Fifth Dimensional Human.

Allow all the blame and judgment that is so easily passed on to you even by those close to you, to wash over you, to slide away from you and set the intent at this level of your awareness to have absolutely all negativity transmuted by the Angels of Light.

Now—release this amber/golden orb of energy from the Root allowing it to travel upwards through your Crown Chakra lodging itself into your 8th Chakra.

Take a deep breath.

At this level, is there anything that you can think of while dwelling within this energy that makes you feel uncomfortable? Now is the time to take note of and work with it. It is a misplaced filament.

Take a deep breath.

Allow this angelic amber/golden orb to ascend—lodging itself within your solar plexus. Using this energy at this level to help you make friends with all of the aspects of the Universal self you still feel incongruent with. Allow this energy to bring into balance all that is needed for you to practice unconditional love by loving the lower and higher Self completely.

Take a deep breath.

Allow this orb of amber/golden light to travel up through the Heart Chakra, pulsating, lodging within the 10th Chakra—the high heart center just above the 8th Chakra. ***This is your Sacred Heart Center.*** Make a commitment this day to do all you humanly can to spread love and enlightenment out into the world, to others. One of the easiest ways of doing this is to connect frequently with the energy of the Heart Center Love Crystals.

Take a deep breath.

Now allow this energy to ascend slowly from the Lower Heart Center—clearing as it transcends the Throat Centre, piercing through to the Third Eye center, through the Crown Center, through the Pyramid of the 8th Chakra, through the Star Triad of the 9th and lodges itself resting at the top of the 10th Chakra. Floating just above the 8th chakra you now have an amber/golden etheric orb of Light which will allow you to work at this particular stage with all that is needed for you to integrate the Spiritual Chakras up to this point and realize the truth of your Angelic/Universal self.

Take a deep breath.

Now bring your attention to the inner silver energy that insulates your etheric membrane, at the fourth-third level of you Aura, as this energy also gives of itself, creating a most beautiful protection and fluidity that manifests as a silver bubble right in the very core of the golden orb.

Take a deep breath.

The golden orb is about 2.5cm in width and about 9cm in diameter and floating within its core is a silver bubble of energy small enough to fit into the orb core. Now, gently lower this orb or light until it fits into the top triangle of the 9th Chakra—at the point of the 8 1/2 Chakra. In other words allow the lower edge of the orb to come to rest on the flat end of the downward pointing triangle that forms part of the star-triad energy within the 9th chakra. In time this will form a support for many other orb energies from the higher charkas, to be birthed within your physical being.

Take a deep breath.

Now visualize within the very core of the silver energy contained within the amber/golden matrix a mother-of-pearl flame about 2.5cm in height, of an iridescent mother-of-pearl vibration. You have the ***platinum flame*** within the iridescent *'mother-of-pearl-like'* vibration at the center of the 9th Chakra and now you have the iridescent *mother-of-pearl flame* within the silver- amber/gold or *relating platinum energy* of the 10th chakra. You are connected to the vibrations and Light of the 10th Chakra, and the activation will begin at its own rate in its own way, naturally.

Know that this is only the beginning stage of activating the powerful energy of the Spiritual Chakras within your physical energy field. Few will accept this energy well.

Others will find it to be a bit intense; either way simply relax into it. If you feel uncomfortable drink some water and feel yourself letting go and merging into it.

Take a deep breath.

Relate to these powerful vibrations emitted from the golden sphere and see how the gold and silver along with the mother-of-pearl energies pulsates light frequencies into the rest of your chakras. First of all begin to visualize these energy orbs of light being transmitted from the 10th Chakra into the 9th, then 8th, then 7th, and so forth all the way down into the Root Center Take your time.

Now visualize how the mother of pearl energy increases in vibration now that the amber/golden and silver energies have laid the foundation for this powerful activation by sparking activity within your auric membranes. Allow the mother-of-pearl energy being emitted by the flame of this center to increase in vibration until your entire energy field vibrates on the frequency of mother-of-pearl.

Now within this powerful transformation of your energy field—claim your authentic angelic Universal Self at one with your human angel.

Claim yourself as a Universal Light worker, a planetary grid-keeper, a divine magical-mystical being that lives in miracles, creates in miracles, and expresses only that which is of the most powerful unconditional love.

In so doing claim yourself as a being who chooses to do, to say, to think and share only that which uplifts others and to do so by practicing forgiveness of the self, claiming yourself as a most powerful being that trusts your Spiritual Ego to guide you instead of allowing the lower ego to take you off guard. Claim yourself as a wonderful emotional being, a sexual being, an earth being that claims the creative orb that is alive within you.

With that, also remember that as a creative being, a multi-dimensional being, no matter the indifferences between you and your family and friends, what matters is for you to continue giving your God-Spark Light to bless them. Allow this energy to be integrated within your being, gently—behind your closed eyes—and see the *Divine Universal Light* moving within you.

Take a deep breath. OPEN your eyes.

Ground yourself-properly anchoring your energy though your Zero Chakras at the balls of the feet into the earth, making sure you are thoroughly grounded. Take three deep breaths. If you feel a swirling or are a bit dizzy, stay put, open your eyes and reach upward with your arms.

Before leaving, make sure that you are fully back into this NOW space.

Exercise for Setting an Intention

Experiencing the fullness of choice is the fuel upon which the soul develops. Choices continually bring to the conscious mind the opportunity to re-evaluate past decisions in light of a wider understanding of life and your purpose. Considering choices provides the opportunity for your next moment of life to exist at a deeper level of intuitive understanding, one that will reflect the greater wholeness of the Universe.

You cannot make a wrong choice within the power of Universal Law *because the reason for your choices is to expand the usable energy of the soul.* Developing your inner *Sanctuary* is the key to expanding this energy on all multi-levels of the body/mind/spirit in a combination form

This means that the available energy for your use in pursuing your spiritual goals is increased when you pay attention to the choices in your life. The greater your willingness to accept the challenges of making those choices, the greater the degree of your Soul Energy and thus the greater degree of the spiritual life force energy that will flow within your body.

The fuel of the soul, the meditative Fifth Dimension energies, exists as a force of change, and if you make certain choices after meditation and tuning in to the direction of your Blessed Higher Self, certain consequences follow. Yet this energy – this force beyond us yet within us – guides us in choosing to experience life in all of its differences, flavors and dimensions, which adds perspective and direction to the ultimate path of learning and purpose for each life time. In other words, the courage to consider choices, and to follow through with your inner decisions, along with the change that inevitably follows, is the power of the life experience and certainly fuels the development of the soul.

Consider this: *Your Soul is a dynamic, growing body of energy, which is responsive to your needs and develops, clears and grows in proportion to the energy, meditation and attention you give it.*

It is impressive to consider the unlimited potential, infinite possibilities and unlimited realities we each possess and the extraordinary opportunities that are presented to us each day. Yet we rarely use these opportunities and often even fail to recognize life's experiences and the possibility of achieving our life desires.

Let's work on how we can create greater clarity in our lives by getting out of our own way. Let's allow the powerful forces of the Universe and Truth govern our lives to help us learn and create our most productive life experiences.

It isn't bad luck or an insensitive Universe that deals you "blows" and obstacles. Rather, it is your own inner motivations, attitudes, and personal beliefs that powerfully influence your life, drawing to you what you expect to receive, and actually may visualize inwardly through your fears. You will receive that which you feel you deserve and that for which you will settle.

Your vulnerabilities and weaknesses become the arenas for optimal change and growth. Problems bring opportunities and Soul growth, depending on how you solve them. Whether a physical disease, financial or family concerns, a deteriorating relationship or unhappiness and dissatisfaction with your job is the issue, the area where you most need to direct your full attention is the one that you would most like to avoid.

While it is natural to avoid the pain of looking into your life and seeing where it doesn't work, this pattern of looking the other way becomes a self-perpetuating excuse to avoid changing what is the source of the pain. It is called denial and is the root of fear. Soul growth begins the willingness to consider your life from a different vantage point, including new perceptions about your life in relation to other people, and in relation to a higher intelligence, which makes room for the fulfillment you most want. This opening brings a chance for the Universe to step in and do its thing – bringing about what you most need to fulfill your desires and step upwards in body, mind and spirit.

When you feel empowered and in control of your life, when things are going smoothly for you, the natural tendency is to coast. When the bottom falls out, when things go wrong, you then pay attention to yourself, your dreams, your fears, and your needs in a very different way. You have nothing to lose by allowing the walls, blocks, fears and obstacles in your life fall away. The fear is the unknown. The hesitancy is to be different from what you have learned and to take a chance on a new way of expression. As you learn to look at your life honestly, increasing your self-awareness, without excuses and defenses, preconceived conditions, you will find the levels of fears and anxiety diminish.

The willingness to re-evaluate the current you and the possibility of creating, with care and understanding, a new you, is what turns limitation into opportunity, destructive old patterning into viable, healthy new pathways for growth and success. Remember every day you live in this lifetime, along with every decision you make and every interaction you share – you are setting up your karma for your next lifetime.

The natural fears of loss, abandonment, death and failure exist just under the surface in our daily living and are triggered by experiences that show us all too clearly our own mortality. These fears can have the effect of causing us to think long and hard about the significance of our life, its meaning and its value. Feeling that we have a purpose and are of value in life is our single most critical need. However, it is very easy in the hurriedness of our lives, to only consider the world in front of us and not look at the entire picture of responses and events. We make mistakes with others and ourselves when we work with EGO, fear, and the *me only* attitude.

Since we all actually exist in a greater dimension of life and have the potential of accessing a greater relationship to an expanded Universe, then it becomes our choice to set the intention as to when we want to begin that journey. We can keep the blinders on and think that life "happens" to us, or we can wake up and begin to understand these energies and learn how to work within and with them to enhance our lives and our future. We either begin this now, in this lifetime, or stay at our birth vibration level and begin again, in another.

When sorting through these opportunities for change and growth, you will find the process painful. We all have thin veneers of self-assurance and wellbeing surrounding us, which cause us to think that our life is under control. When we begin to open to Spirit and realize that the struggle to find meaning, health and happiness is everyone's struggle, then we feel less self- conscious about our difficulties and settle down to a serious and sincere search for the value and meaning of our own lives. The Master said, *"If you do good to even one of my children, you are doing good to me."* If you can save one life during your life span, you have achieved something. To choose to help with many lives through kindness and healing work is Service of the Soul and the Universe.

It is important to have a clear picture of what your current beliefs are about the Universe and your life in relation to this Universe.

Strengthening Your New Aura Meditation

Close your eyes and visualize yourself standing amidst the most rainbow-like beautiful energy.

Take a deep breath.

Visualize yourself standing in the most beautiful amber-golden mist.

It is important to feel very comfortable within this golden energy that takes on the shape of your energy field, beginning to rise up and connect you to your Spiritual Chakras.

Take a deep breath.

See within your mind your Blessed Higher Self, your *Universal Body Self,* contained within the four levels of your Aura, and with that vision—claim yourself to be a powerful being by repeating the *Ascension Invocation for the 8th and 9th Chakra in your mind.* Claim yourself as a powerful healer, creator, and co-creator of this world, working alongside the *One that Creates All,* co-creating your life, your miracles, and your preferred existence upon this plane.

Take a deep breath.

Activate this beautiful amber/golden energy that you are enveloped in as you draw within the power and the strength to practice your intention by accepting the higher energetic vibrations and moving yourself into a whole new power of thought by allowing the Divine Will of the Supreme God Light to be integrated into your entire Universal Being.

Take a deep breath.

Now imagine a most beautiful silver energy manifest on the inside of the amber/golden energy, insulating the three original levels of the Aura, providing amber/golden shield with a liquid silver energy.

Take a deep breath.

Remind yourself that you are an expression of fluid love, as you become the flow of unconditional love towards the Self and all others.

Remind yourself of the feminine aspect of the Universal Body that always supports you in the highest and best way for you to remain flexible, and in so doing, embrace *the Fifth Dimension harmonies*, the flexible side of your personality, by allowing the Creative God Light to ignite within you the energetic vibration that is needed for you to transform your life.

Take a deep breath.

Now connect your heart center energy to the silver and amber/golden energies. If you need to place your hand on your heart to connect to the reality of your pulsating heart do so, once again connect to the pulse of your heart.

Now connect your heart energy to the heart of your etheric plasma, the Universal Body, thus connecting your beating heart to the amber/gold and silver lining around your aura, attached to the 9th Chakra at the back of your head. You do this by sending unconditional love into this area—the part of your physical reality forming your etheric outline—therefore with every beat of your heart, send unconditional love into the spaces that exist between the spaces that surround you. Fill your auric field with this amber/gold and silver light. Send this light-love vibration to fill up all the particles of light that exist between your non-and- physical localities.

Take a deep breath.

Now allow this energy to ascend slowly from the Lower Heart Center—clearing as it transcends the Throat Centre, piercing through to the Third Eye center, through the Crown Center, through the Pyramid of the 8th Chakra, through the Star Triad of the 9th, and lodges itself, resting at the top of the 10th Chakra. Floating just above the 8th chakra, you now have an amber/ golden etheric orb of Light which will allow you to work at this particular stage with all that is needed for you to integrate the Spiritual Chakras up to this point, and realize the truth of your Angelic/Universal self.

Take a deep breath.

Now bring your attention to the inner silver energy that insulates your etheric membrane, at the fourth-third level of your Aura, as this energy also gives of itself, creating a most beautiful protection and fluidity that manifests as a silver bubble right in the very core of the golden orb.

Take a deep breath.

The golden orb is about 2.5 cm in width and about 9 cm in diameter and floating within its core is a silver bubble of energy small enough to fit into the orb core. Now, gently lower this orb or light until it fits into the top triangle of the 9th Chakra—at the point of the 8 1/2 Chakra. In other words allow the lower edge of the orb to come to rest on the flat end of the downward pointing triangle that forms part of the star-triad energy within the 9th Chakra. In time, this will form a support for many other orb energies from the higher charkas to be birthed within your physical being.

Take a deep breath.

Now visualize within the very core of the silver energy contained within the amber/ golden matrix, a mother of pearl flame, about 2.5 cm in height, of an iridescent mother of pearl vibration. You have the ***platinum flame*** within the iridescent *mother-of-pearl* vibration at the center of the 9th Chakra, and now you have the iridescent *mother of pearl flame* within the silver-amber/gold or *relating platinum energy* of the 10th chakra. You are connected to the vibrations and Light of the 10th Chakra and the activation will begin at its own rate in its own way, naturally.

Know that this is only the beginning stage of activating the powerful energy of the Spiritual Chakras within your physical energy field. Few will accept this energy well. Others will find it to be a bit intense; either way, simply relax into it. If you feel uncomfortable drink some water and feel yourself letting go and merging into it.

Take a deep breath.

Relate to these powerful vibrations emitted from the golden sphere and see how the gold and silver along with the mother of pearl energies, pulsate Light frequencies into the rest of your chakras. First of all, begin to visualize these energy orbs of light being transmitted from the 10th Chakra into the 9th, then 8th, then 7th, and so forth all the way down into the Root Center. Take your time.

Now visualize how the mother of pearl energy increases in vibration now that the amber/ golden and silver energies have laid the foundation for this powerful activation by sparking activity within your auric membranes. Allow the mother of pearl energy being emitted by the flame of this center to increase in vibration until your entire energy field vibrates on the frequency of mother of pearl.

As you stand within this powerful transformation of your energy field—claim your authentic angelic Universal Self at one with your human angel. Claim yourself as a Universal Light worker, a planetary gridkeeper, a divine magical-mystical being, that lives in miracles, creates in miracles, and expresses only that which is of the most powerful unconditional love.

In so doing, claim yourself as a being that chooses to do, say, think, and share only that which uplifts others. Do so by practicing forgiveness of the Self, claiming yourself as a most powerful being that trusts your *Spiritual Ego* to guide you instead of allowing the lower ego to take you off guard. Claim yourself as a wonderful, emotional being, a sexual being, an earth being that claims the creative orb that is alive within you. Remember that as a creative being, a multidimensional being, no matter the differences between you and your immediate family and friends, it really doesn't matter. What does matter is for you to continue giving of your God- Spark Light to bless them. Allow this energy to be integrated within your being, gently. Behind closed eyes see the *Divine Universal Light* moving within you.

Take a deep breath. OPEN your eyes.

Ground yourself–properly anchoring your energy though your Zero Chakras at the balls of the feet into the Earth, making sure you are thoroughly grounded. Take three deep breaths. If you feel a swirling or a bit dizzy, stay put, open your eyes and reach upward with your arms. Before leaving, make sure that you are fully back into this NOW space.

END OF MEDITATION

δ

Notes on Oneness Exercises

XIII

Fifth Dimension Definitions

Akashic Records — the non-physical records of all of the past lives one has lived. Also holds the destiny of your soul and your Soul School location. There are Akashic Records for all movement and events that have ever happened in any of the Three Universes. They are filed in alphabetical order by the soul, by Spirit, or your Blessed Higher Self.

Astral Projection — the release of the inner self (etheric body or Universal body) to travel elsewhere – where your thought projects you. Also known as the Out-of-Body Experience. (OBE)

Aura – the energy fields that surround human beings and are seen in various colors. The aura has three levels: physical, emotional, and spiritual. The color patterns that indicate the condition, state of being, health, and level of advancement for the person, plant or animal are visible at all times. The aura changes on a daily basis.

Bi-Location — the ability to be in two or more places at once; either perceived by others or not.

Chakras — the seven psychic organs of the body which are related to the physical organs of the body and run upward along the spine. They are used to direct energy (knowledge) to bring one to various levels of wisdom and understanding.

Energy — (non-physical) the force by which all living matter is composed. It flows at a higher frequency rate than the human body and can be harnessed for healing powers as well as to create levitation.

Energy Patterns — the distinctive configuration of energy that forms the physical and non- physical *State of Being.*

Etheric Body — the other half of you. A non-physical energy within your aura which is attached to you by a silver cord. Also known as the Universal Body, it can soul travel and is the piece of you that experiences the Out of Body sensations. The *etheric/universal body* can be developed to a high degree and can be very helpful to other humans far away or nearby.

Etherically — to become filled with misty light, transparent to the human eye. Not to appear real, but like the ethers.

Guides — spirits of a higher consciousness and greater development who are here to guide us along our life path. Each human alive has two guides with them at all times, usually a male and female. Guides do not have to be with you your entire lifetime and guides can change "stations." As you grow spiritually, the guides change to continually bring you up to a higher level of consciousness. Their function is to bring an incarnate to a deeper level of his spiritual and/or soul development. They may remain with you after death and are assigned to you by the spiritual hierarchy that be.

Harmonization — the alignment of the physical body with the Soul and Universal Body to prepare for Ascension into the Fifth Dimension energies.

Karma — a word from the Eastern philosophies that simply means "action." *For every action there is a reaction.* Used to describe the accumulation of every action you have done in every lifetime you have lived. Basically it says "what goes around comes around" or "whatever you work for or do comes back to you – for good or for ill."

Levitation — the ability to raise and move through thin air. Also to raise objects with your mind. To move something above the earth's surface with thought and without any mechanical means. To defy gravity.

Materialization — the making visible of the invisible. To intensify the energy patterns to make matter out of thin air. Also, the ability of a medium to make things appear in thin air that were invisible beforehand (fire, water, flowers, etc.).

Out Of Body Experience — (OBE) the perceptions that occur while using your Universal body. Occurrences during the time of Astral Travel.

Oversoul — the major *State of Being* – or your *Blessed Higher Self* The higher part of self. When you become one with your oversoul or Blessed Higher Self you dwell within the perfect State of Being. You are complete with yourself for the pursuit of divine development for the growth of the soul. The oversoul has direct contact with the hierarchy of your Soul School as well as angels and the divine saints. It brings you knowledge for your use on the earth plane. It guides you, through thought and new ideas. Depending on the state of advancement of your personal oversoul, it can be capable of those things attributed to deity or miracles. However, it is only a messenger or an instrument to connect you to the powers of the Divine. Your oversoul travels with you during life and after death. It is with you in every lifetime you experience and holds all the information or Akashic Records of your previous lifetimes and all knowledge you have ever learned. It is the "small voice within."

Paranormal — a phenomenon beyond the range of the five senses or of human experience that cannot be explained by scientific means.

Parallel Lives — the process of soul development where one soul can have several lives living at the same time, either all on earth or several lives on several planets.

Past-life Regression — the description of a previous incarnation which usually relates to the current lifetime. You can do a regression yourself or someone can give you a "past-life reading." By experiencing a regression yourself, you "know" from within the facts of the lifetime because you experience it through memory. To be used specifically for healing of fear, disease or trauma.

Post-cognition — knowing about your past without actually living through it. Example: three–year-old boy knows everything there is to know about dinosaurs. Believed to be information brought over from a past life.

Precognition — knowledge of the future. Could be knowledge brought to you by your Blessed Higher Self or a spiritual deity.

Set a Condition — to affirm and pledge to your Blessed Higher Self, Spiritual Guides, and Angels that you will take a certain and specific step to solve a problem or manage your life. It then becomes a covenant with the Universe. Setting a condition helps strongly with manifestation.

Spirit — a non-physical state of conscious being, usually rational and loving; a symbol of the positive, energetic, forceful and formative aspect of the Divine.

Spiritual — denotes the non-physical state or prayer work. It is not connected to any religious ritual or moral code. It is based on the receiver's interpretation and implications.

State Of Being — when one is in the *state of being* through meditation or whatever method, this signifies a place where you are dwelling in the supreme law in the divine realm, of which natural law is the compliment and counterpart. You are perfect in body, mind and spirit. One cannot just go into *the state of being,* as you must progress to get there. The ultimate Self-realization.

State Of Consciousness — a level of awareness experienced by every individual born. You are lifted into higher states of consciousness as the soul develops on the earth plane and fulfills its divine individuality. There are many states of consciousness, 3rd dimensional, 4th dimensional, etc.

Telepathy — the transmitting of thought or ideas from one mind to another. This can be done with thoughts or pictures.

Teleportation — the ability to relocate a body, instantly, from one location to another. This also includes the ability to relocate physical objects by use of the mind only (Star-Trek).

Third Eye — located in the center of the forehead exactly halfway between the brow ridge; this is the 6th Chakra. It is the "seeing" center of the body and its color is indigo. It is the point where all non-physical energy is gathered for knowledge and information. *Both eyes come together as one.* When you open the third eye, you can see.

Universal Consciousness — the knowledge that we all share in a common stream of knowledge and awareness. We are all One.

Vibrations — (Psychic vibrations) energy emanating from spirit, people, animals, objects, and places. Example: We all leave a vibration behind when we leave a chair or a bed. It may take an hour or so for this energy to dissipate. Some people are very sensitive to these vibrations.

About the Author

Elizabeth Joyce

Born as one of two sets of identical twins, Elizabeth Joyce has been psychic since birth. Named one of the *World's Greatest Psychics* (Citadel Press, 2004), she is profiled in twelve books. She is a spiritual healer and gives personal psychic readings worldwide. Ms. Joyce is a professional Astrologer, Spiritual Counselor, Energy Healer, Medium, and Clairvoyant and teaches the new energies of the Fifth Dimension.

Elizabeth has been a writer and columnist for thirty years and is currently writing Astrology columns for *Wisdom Magazine* and *Toti Publishing, as well as several local publications.* Her articles have appeared in the *New York Daily News* and the *New York Times.* She is a spiritual healer and gives personal psychic and energy readings worldwide.

Elizabeth has been teaching metaphysical classes for the past thirty years. She was nominated into the 2010 Edition of the *Stanford Who's Who In Metaphysics* for her Spiritual healing work and focus on Community Service. She is included in the revised book, *America's Top 100 Psychics. (2014)*

Elizabeth has studied with Margaret Stettner, Indira Ivey, Louise Hay, Dr. Deepak Chopra, Yogi Bhajan, Marc Tremblay, and Ammachi, the Hugging Saint.

One of the very few psychics world wide that picked up several well known missing person details, on the Haitian Earthquake, the Philippines earthquake, tornados, and the Twin Towers tragedy in New York City. Thousands of people have witnessed Elizabeth Joyce's incredible psychic powers on TV shows such as *Unsolved Mysteries, Beyond Chance* and *The Psychic Detectives,* as well as *CNN News;* She is a frequent guest on radio shows across the country, including *Coast 2 Coast AM,* with George Noory,

Her website is one of the top-rated in her field. Elizabeth facilitates her own healing classes, using the Divine Seals and Spiritual Chakras from her information books.

Located in Doylestown, PA (Bucks County) Elizabeth works on behalf of more than 30 charities, including Embracing The World, the Red Cross to benefit the Philadelphia area, the homeless, Operation Homefront, supporting the families of our deployed troops, and brushes aside the question of time when pushed for an answer, saying she still has to support non-profit organizations that donate to local charities, such as extra activities for autistic schools and for children with special needs.

Elizabeth's books are available at Amazon.com and her website as well.

Website: *www.new-visions.com*
E-Mail: Elizabeth_joyce@verizon.net
201-934-8986 — 24 hour answering service

Made in the USA
Monee, IL
03 April 2022